Lynched

Lynched

The Power of Memory in a Culture of Terror

Angela D. Sims

BAYLOR UNIVERSITY PRESS

Cover Design by Tim Green, Faceout Studio
Cover image: Tree photograph ©Shutterstock/RHIMAGE

Library of Congress Cataloging-in-Publication Data

Names: Sims, Angela D., author.
Title: Lynched : the power of memory in a culture of terror / Angela D. Sims.
Description: Waco : Baylor University Press, 2017. | Includes bibliographical references and index.
Identifiers: LCCN 2016009312 (print) | LCCN 2016035155 (ebook) | ISBN 9781602582668 (hardback : alk. paper) | ISBN 9781481306072 (web pdf) |ISBN 9781481306065 (mobi) | ISBN 9781481306058 (epub)
Subjects: LCSH: African Americans—Religion. | Lynching—United States—History. | Memory—Moral and ethical aspects. | Terrorism. | Psychology, Religious.
Classification: LCC BR563.N4 S559 2017 (print) | LCC BR563.N4 (ebook) | DDC 364.1/34—dc23
LC record available at https://lccn.loc.gov/2016009312

Printed in the United States of America on acid-free paper with a minimum of 30 percent post-consumer waste recycled content.

Hannah White Allen**Albert David Anderson**Leola Johnson Arnold**Elwood B. Ball**Myrtle Alexander Ballard**Thomas A. Ballard**Lillian J. Blount**Shelton Blount**Addie S. Bolton**Leroy Bowman**David Briggs**J. C. Cain**Margie Kidd Campbell**Odell Poke Carr**Dorothy Sidberry Clark**James Edwin Clark**Julius Dell Coleman**Martin O'Neal Collins**Ola Mae Jackson Comins**Mordessa Richardson Corbin**Freddie Foshee Cudjoe**Donald Wayne Davis**Margaret W. Davis**Jessie Eva Manley Dean**James W. Drakeford**Arthur Dunn**Fannie Wilkinson Fitzgerald**Rodger Pierpont Fitzgerald**Katherine Louise Clark Fletcher**Nazzaree Williams Franklin**Olive Lee Joyner**Nims Edward Gay Jr.**Theresa Jackson Gilliam**Josephine Green**George M. Hampton**Sarah Lee Robinson Hardimon**Artie L. Harris**Marguerite B. Harris**Wallace S. Hartsfield Sr.**Gwendolyn Elaine Brown Hill**Ireland Hill**Zan Holmes**Lettie Ruth Cooper Hunter**Katherine Coleman Goble Johnson**Leon Johnson**Shirley Johnson**Ann Jones**John Jones**Lucille Otis Jones**Julia K. Gibson Jordan**Rosalie Hilliard Joseph**Clarence Walter Kidd**Emma Atkins Kidd**

With immense gratitude to African American elders whose oral history accounts make this project possible

L. P. Lewis**Lillian McDonald Marigny**Solon Marshall**Benjamin Franklin Martin**Anita Earnest McCohn**Godfrey McCray**Willie McLean**Eva Partee McMillan**Carrie Lee Thornton Miller**Lois Louise Donaldson Miller**Janie Montgomery**Ora Lee Bland Morgan**Simon W. Morgan**Junius Warren Nottingham**Ellie Winfield Palmer**Collier Parks Jr.**Ollie Roberta Pearson**Lillie Phenix**Helen Swazer Pollard**Brelon Price**Joseph Purvis**William Samuel Randolph**Maggie Thornton Renfro**Claretha Robinson**Barbara Rollins**Catherine Thompson Sidney**John A. Sims**Rebecca Brown Singleton**Betty Spencer**King Swazer Jr.**Dorothy London Thomas**George Leon Thomas**Willie Matthew Thomas**Hazel Lee Peoples Thompson**Leon Thompson Jr.**Mary G. Clark Thompson**Sadie Watson Todd**Bozie Mae Flemings Walker**Ella Mae Warren**Lovie Warren**Rosie Lee Thornton Warren**Louis Lee White Sr.**Earl Williams Sr.**Ulysses Samuel Williams**

Contents

Acknowledgments

G rateful acknowledgement is made to the following institutions that provided financial support for this project:

2009–2010 General Program Grant from the Louisville Institute

2010 Wabash Summer Research Fellowship from the Wabash Center for Teaching and Learning in Theology and Religion

2010–2011 Visiting Scholar for the Womanist Scholars Program at the Interdenominational Theological Center

2010–2011 Ford Foundation Postdoctoral Fellowship

I am extremely thankful to Dr. Stephen Sloan, Director, The Institute for Oral History at Baylor University, along with his staff (especially Becky Shulda and Elinor Mazé) for training in oral history methodology and equipment usage as well as countless hours dedicated to transcribing and editing interviews. In addition, Terry L. Goodrich, Assistant Director of Media Communications at Baylor University, devoted numerous hours to promote the oral history project "Remembering Lynching: Strategies of Resistance and Visions of Justice." Almost from the inception of this research, Dr. Carey C. Newman, Director, Baylor University Press, has shepherded my work. I am deeply grateful for his probing questions, professionalism, and friendship.

I owe special thanks to Kazz Alexander Pinkard, Larry Williams, and Janise Randall for technical and research support. I am grateful to Mrs. Carolyn Frederick, Mrs. Deloris Randolph, Reverend Dr. Barbara Morton, Reverend Veronica Thomas, Reverend Dr. Helen Byrd, Reverend Dr. Victor McCullough, Ms. Rachel McClain, Ms. Vickie Washington, Dr. Evelyn Parker, Mrs. Glorious Ford, Reverend Demetrics Roscoe, Mrs. Rhonda Lyle, and Reverend Dr. Luke E. Torian for assistance in advertising the oral history project, recommending names of potential participants, and offering the use of space in which to conduct interviews.

I am privileged to work at Saint Paul School of Theology in Overland Park, Kansas, and Oklahoma City, Oklahoma. My colleagues, in conjunction with the Board of Trustees, approved and granted me a fall 2010 research leave and a spring 2011 sabbatical. As a result, their generosity and willingness to relieve me from teaching and committee responsibilities allowed me to concentrate full time on this writing project. I also want to thank David Firman, whose administrative support alleviated any concerns associated with an almost eleven-month absence from Kansas City and who printed multiple versions of this manuscript. Though they are no longer affiliated with Saint Paul School of Theology, I am most appreciative of Dr. Pamela Couture and Dr. Myron

McCoy, for their willingness to write letters of endorsement in support of my research.

Family and friends offered support and encouragement from the time I began to imagine this oral history project. Dr. Renee K. Harrison and Dr. Z. Hall read multiple iterations of several chapters. Their constructive feedback was invaluable. A few sister-friends—Margaretta Narcisse, Cynthia Adams, Jerlys Coles, Doris Morelock Hendrickson, AnneMarie Mingo, Sharon Nottingham, Maudry Orphy, Sylvia Perry, Alice Snyder, Jennifer Thompson, S'thembile West, and Phyllis York—deserve special recognition. Special thanks to Dr. Katie Geneva Cannon, Dr. Emilie M. Townes, Dr. Stephen Ray, Dr. Stacey Floyd-Thomas, Dr. Patricia Beattie Jung, Dr. Nancy Howell, and Dr. Elaine Robinson for their commitment to mentor and for their gentle, and sometimes not so gentle, nudging me to do the work. Finally, I thank God for my spouse, my children, my granddaughter, and our circle of family who pray with and for me and remind me frequently to care for myself.

Preface

We knew where we was supposed to be,
and we didn't bother.

—Leola Arnold

 he July 2010 firing of Mrs. Shirley Sherrod by the secre-
tary of agriculture—for remarks she made at an NAACP
banquet[1] in which she reflected on a defining moment that
caused her to recognize that poverty was not a respecter
of persons—presented her an opportunity to discuss her
father's lynching. Though Sherrod did not use the term
"lynching" to describe her father's brutal murder (which did
not result in an indictment, let alone a conviction, of the persons who committed this crime), her narrative reminds me
of the urgency associated with my oral history project to document and preserve lynching narratives of African Americans who lived during an era when domestic terror was an
almost unquestioned practice. Without question, I have a

tremendous responsibility to honor the integrity of the narratives entrusted to my care. At the same time, I realize that a contextualized ethical-theological analysis demands that I engage in a "thick description" if I am to articulate how various strategies of resistance, consciously or not, informed a hope-filled future that many participants attribute to their faith in Jesus, the resurrected Christ.

Themes of external and internal patterns of migration and the various ways in which persons negotiated real and/ or imagined borders function as indicators to understand the role of formal and informal education and the diverse ways in which faith is lived out on a daily basis. Since graduate theological education is not a prerequisite for ministerial credentialing in my own religious tradition, themes related to formal and informal education may serve to remind persons of the tremendous sacrifices of African Americans, and those with whom they were aligned, and in so doing compel us to be more deliberate to become adept in our ability to interpret messages often disguised to distort a presenting moral problem.

Sherrod knew, from a young age, that she would be, in a manner likened to late nineteenth- and early twentieth-century anti-lynching advocate Ida B. Wells, on a "crusade for justice." Sherrod's ability to name a problem correctly, to assess a situation from multiple perspectives, to confront her own biases, and to "count the costs" that may inevitably call into question a person's ability to "stay the course" when confronting culturally entrenched sin suggests not only that she *knew where she was supposed to be* but also that she did not feel compelled to ask permission from self-appointed power brokers to affirm her determination to make a difference in the lives of those who often found their backs pressed against walls of injustice.

Although some sources record only two lynchings of African Americans in 1939, the latest year a "Remembering Lynching" participant would have been born, African American lynching narratives indicate that this cultural practice continued to function as a metaphor to control human behavior. Persons who came of age during this reign of terror had to, as a matter of survival, *know where they were supposed to be* and, at the same time, not be driven by internalized fear to an extent that they were paralyzed into inactivity. This ability to navigate spaces that were subject to detonate without warning demanded an attention to social nuances, communication patterns, and interpersonal interaction. This skill set was for many of the United States' black citizens, whether acknowledged or not, an essential aspect of life. Called to an active faith, irrespective of religious orientation, that compelled them to become creative architects, African Americans who remember lynching designed responses that were antithetical to imposed ways of being in order to imagine and affirm an alternative reality from which emerged life-affirming messages.

Given a growing media trend to disregard context in order to characterize selected comments about experiences in the United States—for instance, as racist or anti-patriotic—African American elders' lynching narratives offer another glimpse into techniques that enabled persons of moral courage to stare hatred in the face and not to be consumed or defined by dehumanizing behavior. These primary sources, a complement to existing ethical-theological materials, emerge from and are informed by a particular historical period with yet unfolding contemporary implications. These are not sound

bites. Instead, these oral histories are a snapshot into intricacies associated with archival data extraction that, in several
instances, has not been accessed in years. As such, African
American lynching narratives are part of a canon of work that
challenges us to consider what is required of us if our embodied actions are to convey that we are, at both a personal and a
communal level, socially responsible global citizens.

1

Echoes of a Not So Distant Past

African Americans Remember Lynching

From July 2009 to February 2011, I recorded oral histories with persons who live in Alexandria, Ashland, Dumfries, Hampton, Newport News, Norfolk, Occoquan, and Woodbridge (Virginia); Sumter (South Carolina); Hillside, Linden, and Roselle (New Jersey); Omaha (Nebraska); Kansas City (Missouri); Oklahoma City (Oklahoma); Dallas and Richardson (Texas); Benton, Bossier City, Gilbert, Lake Charles, Minden, Monroe, Shreveport, and Winnsboro (Louisiana); Berkeley, Emeryville, Hayward, Lafayette, and Oakland (California); Philadelphia (Pennsylvania); and Birmingham (Alabama). Colleagues, relatives, friends, and well-meaning others often want to know how I can stand to read about lynching. Given the nature of this grotesque form of inhumanity, a few inquire out of concern that I not internalize rage associated with this work. At the same time, some suggest that lynching, particularly when understood narrowly as death by hanging without due process of law, is irrelevant and of little concern to a large sector of the population. These were not concerns I had in mind when I began to imagine an oral history project to document narratives of African Americans who were at least seventy years old. However, I did have questions. In particular, I wanted the participants to discuss (a) why people do or do not talk about lynching and what it means, (b) how lynching or a culture of lynching shapes their understanding of justice and faith in God, and (c) their concerns and desires for future generations. A majority of the more than fifty participants from my "Remembering Lynching: Strategies of Resistance and Visions of Justice" project responded to my queries. All the participants also provided biographical data to contextualize their narratives. In many respects, particularly as I listen to their oral histories and read the transcripts, their act of remembering becomes a point of entry from which to examine personal-corporate practices of sacred social ritualization.

For participants, to remember is an intentional act to decide what to do with suppressed, denied, or ignored memory when it is couched in violence. To remember is an opportunity to document their lived experiences as resources for future generations. To remember is also an opportunity for some to give voice to an eschatological hope that the church, a body of baptized believers who proclaim that Jesus is the Christ, the son of the true and living God, will live into its communion of eucharistic promise. This intentionality to recall raises another set of questions that these oral histories evoke. Examination of a biblical invitation to gather, to commune, to bear witness to Jesus' lived experience calls forth concerns about whether we remember because we are baptized or whether baptism is an ethical imperative to remember acts of injustice and act justly.

Baptism by immersion, one of two ordinances observed by Baptists, is a time of communal celebration that is witnessed by family, friends, and other caring individuals. Regardless of age, this rite of passage signals a baptism candidate's fidelity to God through a profession of faith in Jesus the Christ, and it conveys, at least in theory, full privileges of church membership. Many baptismal candidates in my faith tradition, at least from my experience, receive minimal advance instruction on the actual immersion process. This translates, quite literally, to an element of trust in the baptismal process and the officiant's proficiency with this sacramental act. Swimming proficiency and phobias are dispelled, at least for a few minutes, as candidates step into the water and entrust themselves into the officiant's care. It is in this moment that faith-informed trust lends itself to a transformation of water into a ritual of baptism. This sacred act is a public declaration that solidifies a community's commitment to live in relationship with all of creation in a manner that reflects its relationship with a triune God. When viewed metaphorically, this process of sacred social ritualization can be problematic for persons who came of age in the United States during a period marked by a reign of terror.

When I launched the "Remembering Lynching" project, I had spent almost six years examining historical-contemporary ethical dimensions of lynching. I realized within days of the initial interviews that there was something about the very character of oral history that captured and held my attention, though not without some necessary procedural adaptations. An e-mail from a friend a few days before my first interview expressed concern for my emotional and spiritual wellness as I embarked upon this phase of my research. This message should have served as an indicator that change was inevitable as I stepped both into the water and into the memories. Just as baptismal candidates are given brief instructions on breathing techniques and how to position their bodies in the water, I realized quickly that I had a moral responsibility to offer some guidance—beyond ensuring each participant understood the project's focus and my research methodology[1]—that would enable us to be submersed but not overwhelmed by archived memories.

Before I traveled to the Washington, D.C., metropolitan area in July 2009 to begin fieldwork, the ethical-theological dimension of baptism's relevance to this oral history project's hypothesis[2] or research and interview questions[3] was not even a peripheral thought. Without question, I would have to cross-reference each interview to determine if, or how frequent, baptism is even mentioned in the "Remembering Lynching" oral history collection. Irrespective of their faith tradition's theological position on baptism,[4] I would not be surprised if participants do not concur with me that their act of remembering lynching is akin to a process of sacred social ritualization, particularly baptism. At the same time, I am not compelled to convince any of the African American elders who entrusted their narratives to me about my subsequent post–field-research assertion. Rather, I want to thank them for granting me a small glimpse into their memories about lynching and a culture of lynching—a glimpse that often reminded me and others, such as my primary videographer Kazz Alexander Pinkard, that the past is not nearly as distant as we might wish.

As I listened to then ninety-year-old Deacon James Drakeford, with tears streaming down his face, recall childhood stories told to him by his formerly enslaved grandfather, I realized the significance of my friend's e-mail. Drakeford was born fifty-three years after the official end of chattel slavery in the United States of America, and his response was a clear indicator that I had not considered that a discussion of lynching and a culture of lynching might also trigger memories of transmitted slave narratives. I also had not factored in the range of emotions that a discussion about lynching and a culture of lynching might elicit. In subsequent conversations with my friend who e-mailed to say she was praying with and for me as I began this oral history project, I realized she knew then—as I sat in a living room in Ashland, Virginia, on July 15, 2009—what I was only beginning to realize. I was on a journey of discovery that demanded I navigate memories with care—that I listen attentively, demonstrate respect, and connect on a personal level so that I could bring closure to our time of sharing in a life-affirming manner. Together, "Remembering Lynching" contributors and I engaged in a process analogous to a process of submersion whereby the act of remembering is symbolized as a ritual of baptism—not a literal baptism by water, but a symbolic immersion that plunged and invited me to journey with participants into repressed, suppressed, reconfigured, and ritualized memories as they remembered lynching and a culture of lynching: an immersion that recalled various strategies of resistance from which they and others imagined the unfolding of God's creation that invites each of us to be doers of justice. However, in order to embody this dimension of our baptismal informed communion, how we understand an act of remembering influences how we interpret and subsequently appropriate the frequency and manner in which we *eat this bread and drink the cup* as well as how we *proclaim the Lord's death until he comes.*

I do not analyze "Remembering Lynching" narratives against a scriptural text. Instead, I use these oral histories to investigate lynching as a social-cultural-religious phenomenon. As primary sources, these narratives inform an ethical-theological analysis of remembering. Participants' earliest memories of lynching coupled with why persons choose to (or not) discuss lynching are repositories that illustrate with clarity that historical interpretation is always incomplete, or as an excerpt imprinted on a banner at the opening of Alice Walker's papers at Emory University highlighted, "history is a keeping of records."[5] Yet, from these intentional and otherwise cautionary narratives, a process of ritualization associated with earliest memories of lynching and justifications for discussing (or not) this heinous social spectacle evokes several questions about historical recall as a metaphor for baptism. As each African American elder *stepped into the water to be baptized*—to recall a time in history when, as Martin Collins recalled, "it was nothing they could much do . . . that was the process back then . . . that was the way they did things"[6]—the elder's very action became a lens through which to examine the function of suffering servant and turn the other cheek when posited as Christian virtues. In its deeper significance, however, these two motifs ask Christians to evaluate what it means to be church. This is of particular importance given that baptism is not necessarily synonymous with a capacity to remember. Furthermore, these two motifs invite Christians to explore how a capacity to remember may expand our stance on who is called to remember.

Socio-Historical Consciousness:
"Don't know anything about it"

For several Sundays during early spring 2009, St. Stephen Baptist Church in Kansas City, Missouri, posted, in their bulletin, an announcement about my oral history project, "Remembering Lynching: Strategies of Resistance and Visions of Justice." St. Stephen, a historically black church, was founded four decades after President Abraham Lincoln signed the Emancipation Proclamation. A review of St. Stephen's history[7] offers insights about and responses to racial policies operative in Kansas City and other sectors of the United States from the early 1950s to the mid-1980s. For instance, St. Stephen's fourth pastor, Dr. Mac Charles Jones (remembered as a "courageous leader"[8] for his commitment to justice), led the National Council of Churches National Ministries, which included racial justice work and response to arson attacks on churches.[9] Not only did Jones seek creative ways to confront the Ku Klux Klan in 1984 in his hometown, LaGrange, Georgia; but also he traveled internationally to address human rights issues.[10]

Given this legacy of communal-social justice engaged awareness, I expected several St. Stephen members to share their memories about lynching and a culture of lynching with me. After all, a quick scan of the congregation on any given Sunday suggested that a majority of worshippers were at least seventy years old. In addition, from conversations with several senior members, I knew that some of them had migrated to Kansas City from various southern locales to further their educations and/or pursue nonagricultural careers. I also assumed that lifelong residents of the Kansas City metropolitan area would have some recollection of stories transmitted across generations about a hanging tree in the Westport section of Kansas City. I thought it possible that some would recall memories of ten well-documented lynchings that occurred in Cass, Clay, Jackson, and Platte Counties, between 1869 and 1925. These four counties now comprise Kansas City.[11] When it became apparent no one would respond to the announcement, I approached several individuals to invite them personally to participate in this ethical-historical project. From each I received the same response: "I don't know anything about that." I concluded that the St. Stephen members' decisions not to participate in my study may point to distinctions between public and private responses to moral issues. This is made clearer in Mrs. Hazel Lee Peoples Thompson's responses to my query about her earliest memory of lynching.

Thompson spent her formative years in a small rural town in Bienville Parish in southeast Louisiana. Born March 25, 1932, in Saline, Thompson grew up on land owned and worked by her father. Thompson's comments about land-ownership and sharecropping may point to ways in which socio-class distinctions inform concepts about violence. Although there are documented accounts of lynching in Bienville Parish from as early as May 15, 1881, to February 19, 1933, approximately a year after Thompson's birth,[12] her initial response about her earliest recollection of lynching was, "Well, I really don't know anything about it because as I say, my daddy had his own place."[13] It is also possible that Thompson's association of lynching with sharecropping or for-hire farm labor practices was informed by a tradition of *knowing* shrouded intentionally in *silence* as a strategy to deter unwanted attention. Unlike her spouse, Thompson stated she didn't "know anything about working for the white man like he's[14] talking about. I worked my daddy's farm, but he had his own—we went and did what we had to do. I mean it wasn't no white man involved. But I really don't know what happened or how you would work in the field with white people."[15] Perhaps Thompson's parents and adults with whom they interacted did not discuss lynchings that took place in Bienville Parish and other locales as reported in newspapers, particularly Negro weeklies,[16] with their children. It is quite possible their *silence* allowed them to exercise agency as they determined ways to shield their children from the horrors of domestically sanctioned terror. Whatever the reasons "parents never discussed things like that,"[17] Thompson's initial response about lynching is not an anathema. For as Alice Walker recounts in *The Same River Twice*, "Nobody talks about the lynched."[18]

Disassociated Geographical Connections: "Never close around my hometown"

Dubbed "Crossroads" of the Gulf Coast, Victoria, Texas, sits thirty miles inland from the Gulf of Mexico. As the principal town in a predominately farming and ranching region, Victoria's growth remained steady until the 1930s and 1940s, when the development of the petroleum industry and the establishment of army air bases sharply changed the economic complexity of the town. The first sustained producing oil well for Victoria County became a reality at the McFaddin Ranch in the early 1930s, resulting in the emergence of thriving petroleum-related enterprises.[19]

Born in Victoria, Texas, on March 30, 1919, Ireland Hill grew up within approximately a two-hour drive of Austin, Corpus Christi, Houston, and San Antonio. When Hill reflected in January 2010 on his earliest memory of lynching, he recounted that adults "didn't talk too much about it because it wasn't ever close around my hometown about anyone who was lynched." Even if lynching did not occur within the immediate vicinity of Victoria, it stands to reason Hill knew about this cultural phenomenon. As he explained, "Now and again you'd hear them say a few words, but they didn't talk too much about it."[20]

Although Hill did not elaborate about what he heard, his succinct comments suggest that conversations about practices designed especially to control human behavior were not something that African Americans engaged in openly. During a time when individuals did not have to *die at the hands of persons unknown*[21] and known or be threatened verbally or physically with loss of life to achieve a desired socio-behavioral outcome, Hill remembered,

> We knew exactly what to do if we went to town. You know, you stayed your distance—whatever you wanted to do you did it—back in the colored part of the town. But in my little town it was a lot of ranches and oil wells and things. And most of the people in that little town was rich. So we didn't have too much dealing with them. Because most of them were—you know, they had the servants. I think they had thirteen millionaires that lived in that little town—all white—all ranchers[22]—so we didn't come in contact—they didn't come in contact with us too much. And we didn't come in contact with them too much. So—and then I—we never did stay on anybody's place, you know, sharecrop. We didn't—our grandpa had quite a bit of land and he built every one of his sons a new home.[23]

Like Hazel Lee Peoples Thompson, Hills seems to connect, to some degree, correlations of lynching to land ownership or, more specifically, to share cropping or labor-for-hire.

It is virtually impossible, though, to estimate how spoken and unarticulated codes of conduct factored in reducing incidents of physical lynching while simultaneously ensnaring all citizens in a system of violence. After all, while indicators of mob rule may not have been readily apparent in Victoria, Hill's recollections suggest there was something operative within the town's culture that compelled adults to discuss lynching. Otherwise, it would not have been necessary for Hill and other "coloreds" to know how to conduct themselves outside of their prescribed community. Without addressing this country's national sin, Hill and others benefitted from a tradition that equipped them to navigate potential encounters with violence as a way to safeguard and preserve life and property.

In his sociological analysis of the United States' fascination with terror, Arthur F. Raper reports that during the first three decades of the twentieth century, Texas had a (reported)[24] lynching rate of 2.5 per ten thousand of the African American population.[25] From 1900 until 1919, the year of Hill's birth, newspapers documented at least eleven Texas lynchings. On March 13, 1901, almost eighteen years before Hill was born, "John Henderson, the negro accused of murdering Mrs. Younger, was burned at the stake by a mob of 5,000 persons in Corsicana, Texas. He purportedly had confessed his guilt. Subsequently, the coroner held an inquest over his remains and the jury returned a verdict commending the mob for its act of horror."[26] The following year, "Dudley Morgan, a Negro accused of assailing Mrs. McKay, wife of a Section Foreman was burned to death at an iron stake in Lansing, Texas on May 23, 1902. A crowd of 4,000 men, most of whom were armed, snatched him from the officers on the arrival of the train."[27] The following year, a mob "began terrifying the colored residents of Whitesboro" on August 12, 1903, after police intercepted a lynching in progress.[28] Seven years later on July 31, 1910, "at least fifteen and perhaps as many as twenty negroes, all of them probably unarmed, were hunted down and killed by a mob of 200 or 300 men in the Slocum and Denison Springs neighborhood of Palestine. Sheriff Black said today that the Negroes were killed 'without any real cause at all.' "[29]

In 1913, within a two-hour drive of Victoria, Texas, "a mob of 1,000 persons conducted a mock trial in the courthouse yard in Houston, found David Rucker, negro, aged 30, guilty of murdering Mrs. J. C. Williams, and, in the presence of a sheriff and two deputies who were powerless to act, chained him to a steel pump in the middle of the yard, soaked his clothes with oil, piled wood about him and burned him alive on February 8th."[30] Between February 9, 1913, and Hill's March 30, 1919, birth, there are at least seven recorded lynchings: two in Marshall on February 24, 1913;[31] one in Beaumont on June 6, 1913;[32] another in Marshall on April 29, 1914;[33] one in Angleton on October 15, 1914;[34] the infamous Waco May 15, 1916, burning death witnessed by approximately 15,000 men, women, and children;[35] and on October 12, 1917, "eight hundred oil-field-workers—whites, Mexicans, Germans and Italians—employed at Goose Creek, a suburb of Houston, seized Bert Smith, a member of the Race and brutally hung him to a tree and riddled his body with bullets and horribly mutilated it with sledge-hammers and butcher knives after cutting it down."[36]

Recorded accounts of known lynchings may support Hill's assertion that persons were not subjected to *southern horrors* in or near Victoria. However, evidence from the *Kansas City Times* (Missouri), *New York Negro World, New York*

Sun, Baltimore Herald, New York Herald, New York Call, Brooklyn Citizen, New York World, New York Globe, Wilmington Advocate (Delaware), *New York News,* and *Pittsburg American*[37] indicate that this fascination with death at the hands of known and unknown persons continued, virtually unchecked, for years in numerous locales, including Houston, approximately a two-hour drive from Victoria. In 1930, when Hill was about eleven years old, twenty-one persons were reported lynched in the United States. Three of these were in Texas.[38] The Sherman Riot in 1930, however, was a notable example of racial violence committed by a mob.[39] After 1930, there was never more than one mob a year.[40] Six years without a lynching preceded the final clear-cut case, the lynching of accused rapist William Vinson at Texarkana on July 13, 1942,[41] one or two years after Hill migrated from Victoria, Texas, to Oakland, California. Even if lynching was "never close around Hill's hometown," vigilante activity in Texas predated his 1919 birth, with numerous incidents documented during the at least twenty-one years Hill resided in Texas. In addition, James Byrd's June 7, 1998, lynching by dragging in Jasper, Texas,[42] challenges us to be more attentive to our surroundings so that we can, individually and collectively, work to ensure that lynching will become a historical marker that points us toward a more just tomorrow.

Selective Transmission across Generations: "Something that just wasn't talked about"

We could interpret Alice Walker's declaration "no one talks about the lynched"[43] to imply that victims' survivors rarely challenge stories of atrocities committed by cowards who abused a self-designed legal system. We might also conclude that persons may have decided, for various reasons, to suppress their memories of lynching. It is even possible that the manner in which historical events are transmitted may inform how persons both recall traumatic incidents and draw correlations to contemporary realities.

When Jessie Eva Manley Dean, born March 8, 1925, in Nansemond County, reflected on her earliest memory of lynching, she said, "I never learned anything about lynching until I read about it." When it came to lynching, Dean, who attended and graduated from Nansemond County public schools prior to relocating to Norfolk and after she graduated from high school, explained that before she entered second or third grade she "didn't know anything. Oh, you know what, when I read about it, this was during Black History, when they would speak of it in school."[44]

Dean's memory of lynching and a culture of lynching is connected not to twentieth-century lynchings in Virginia[45] or other sectors of the United States but to Nat Turner.[46] It is quite possible this can be attributed in part to Virginia's 1928 anti-lynching law,[47] acclaimed at the time as the United States' "most forceful statement against mob law."[48] While this legislation may have contributed to a decline in deaths, it did not ameliorate white supremacy, disguised as paternalism, which undergirded a system of racial inequalities.[49]

Less than fifty miles from now extinct Nansemond,[50] Nat Turner was born in Southampton, Virginia, on October 2, 1800. A few months before his thirty-first birthday, Turner organized and led a slave rebellion that resulted in multiple deaths and culminated in his execution by hanging and skinning.[51] It was this narrative of rebellion against a caste system of perpetual enslavement that Dean remembered. As she recalled,

Now, Nat Turner, they spoke of him because he was not too far from where I lived in Nansemond County. He was in Southampton County, and I guess that stuck with me more so than any other lynching that I read or the teacher taught us. Because they would say, "Nat Turner, he's from Southampton County." And that was near Franklin, Virginia,[52] so you know, you keep this in mind because it was so close. And they would tell, you know, how he killed people or how he killed so many and what he did. And that went over and over and over and it stayed in my mind because it was so close. Now, any other lynching that they taught us or spoke about, it just went in one ear and out the other. But this particular lynching about Nat Turner and all of that he did, it just stuck with me because—I would think about it at night, you know, because it was so close. Southampton County is right close, you know. And his lynching stuck with me more so when I was a child than any other.[53]

Interestingly, as the youngest of her parents' nine daughters, Dean had no recollection of her North Carolina–born father speaking with his wife or other adults about individuals who were killed without benefit of due process of law.

What Dean's primary association of lynching with a documented event of socio-political insurrection that occurred almost a century before her birth does is to raise questions about the manner in which associative memory is a process of socialization. All too often, as Dean's earliest memory of lynching suggests, a national narrative can be constructed as either a dominant or a singular historical-social reference point. For some individuals, this may preclude an ability to question cultural mores as well as inhibit an ability to engage in relevant historical contemporary comparisons. Although the hangman's knot was the operative form of capital punishment in the nineteenth century, it is imperative not to conflate Nat Turner's death with lynching. This is not to suggest that capital punishment, even as practiced in a sterile prison chamber replete with intravenous equipment and a spectators' gallery, cannot function as a literal and metaphorical representation of lynching. Rather, given what we know about the systemic nature of injustice in the United States, I caution this comparative analysis that centers Nat Turner as an example of lynching. Such an emphasis may unintentionally conflate all forms of capital punishment with extrajudicial killings. Of concern is a manner in which language can be employed to minimize the gravity of lynching and the countless lives forever disrupted as a result of this practice. At the same time, associative memory as a function of collective indoctrination emphasizes the significance of oral history as a function of Christian moral discernment. At the very least, Thompson's, Hill's, and Dean's recollections of lynching suggest that selective transmissions of a national dilemma across generations compels us not to assume that we know what constitutes *good news*. Daily, we must ask ourselves not what is this gospel of Jesus the Christ but how does this incarnational narrative inform the manner in which we seek to remember that which epitomizes evil as we simultaneously strive to embody that which is just.

Historical Detachment:
"Don't want to be reminded of what took place"

It has been said that fiction can depict reality in a manner that often diminishes consequences that sometimes accompany truth telling. While Mrs. Lucille Otis Jones, like most individuals whom I interviewed during June 2009 and February

2011, did not witness a lynching, she associates her earliest memory of this form of torture with the cinema, a form of entertainment that may, on the one hand, desensitize and, on the other hand, raise individual and communal awareness. Jones, born March 3, 1929, in Franklin, Louisiana, recalls her earliest memory as seeing

> the movie—what you call it—Ku Klux Klan? That's where I really began to hear different things by the Ku Klux Klan, because the Ku Klux Klan was rough. You know what I mean? I heard that. The movie, they showed that. Then when they would have little old building made, tie a rope around your neck and step on the rope or something; they'd pop their neck. I remember that.[54]

Regardless of how it is depicted in the movies, the Ku Klux Klan was anything but a creative work of writers' and directors' imaginations. As I note in *Ethical Complications of Lynching: Ida B. Wells's Interrogation of American Terror*, the Ku Klux Klan, established in Tennessee in 1865, described itself as an institution of chivalry, humanity, mercy, and patriotism. In actuality it was a domestic terrorist organization with the express intent to maintain and reestablish white supremacy in the South through every kind of intimidation and violence against black people and their supporters.[55] Though the Ku Klux Klan did not exist in Louisiana during the years immediately following the abolition of slavery, the Knights of the White Camelia, established in Jones' hometown in 1867, served a similar purpose.[56]

Like the Ku Klux Klan, the Knights of the White Camelia was a secret society with elaborate ceremonies, signs, rituals, and passwords and, more importantly, an avowedly racist

purpose.[57] Because of its racist appeal, the secret society was
an immediate and unqualified success. With no restrictions
or limits imposed on their activities, chapters were organized
throughout the state, as whites rallied in response to the
black political assault on the social status quo. Most of the
rural membership, however, lived in the Acadian parishes,[58]
which includes St. Mary, whose parish seat is Franklin. Disappointed by the outcome of the 1868 presidential election,
most Knights of the White Camelia left the organization,
and by mid-1869 the terrorist group had ceased to exist.[59] In
its stead, hate groups such as the Bayou Knights of the Ku
Klux Klan,[60] Louisiana White Knights of the Ku Klux Klan,[61]
National Aryan Knights of the Ku Klux Klan,[62] and Southern
Knights of the Ku Klux Klan[63] emerged and continue, unfortunately, a legacy of inferiority-induced evil that affects ultimately the well-being of all citizens.

As I listened to Jones' memories of lynching, it became
apparent that, while her narrative shared characteristics that
some might associate with the literary genre of historical fiction, her recollection of a society that produced and tolerated
this inhumane treatment was informed by her own knowledge and awareness of cultural practices in rural Franklin,
Louisiana, whose primary agricultural crop was sugarcane.[64]
With regard to unexplained disappearances, Jones recalled,
"Well, have some people come up missing, didn't know that
happened to them. You know what I mean? Traveling by
night; so yeah I heard about people come up missing." She
mentioned that adults in her community also talked about
individuals who were killed for no reason. According to Jones,

> [My] parents never did talk to us, that in front of us,
> because they know we was chicken; I mean chicken

scared, you know? But we always had to be careful where we go and what we say. Well, with the way those people, the Ku Klux Klan—they didn't like you black folks. Anything they can do to get to you, they'll get to you; and especially to see a black man with a white woman. That's when the whole stuff come in at. But it was all right for the white man to be with a black woman. See, now I know that for a fact.

Given these circumstances, Jones explained that her parents provided indirect survival instruction to their four children.

Without discussing the nuances of a present danger, her parents instructed Jones and her sister and two brothers "to be careful, what we say and where we go because there was a crook, there was a crook. Out there in the country, it had a cane field, and that's the thing you had to watch. Because they can drag you in them cane fields down there, you know? You wouldn't know what be done happened to you. They would do that—they sure would do that because the white man, you know."[65] Although Jones did not provide evidence to support this cautionary advice to avoid cane fields, one need only read Laura Wexler's *Fire in a Canebrake: The Last Mass Lynching in America*[66] to grasp the significance of Jones' description of an aspect of life in Franklin, Louisiana, in the early to middle twentieth century. For Jones and others, life often depended on an ability to be aware constantly of their surroundings.

Fear-Induced Silence: "Culture of fear still exists"

A memory of lynching, the act itself a form of domestic terror that continues to function symbolically as a mechanism by which to control human behavior, is, consciously or not, for many African American elders who are now at least seventy-six years old, a defining moment. Recovering and preserving these narratives that have, in one too many instances, been silenced for decades necessitates that we acknowledge that a culture of fear is still prevalent in the United States of America. As theologian and philosopher Howard Thurman noted, "When the external circumstances of life are dramatic or unusual, causing the human spirit to make demands upon all the reaches of its resourcefulness in order to keep from being engulfed, then the value of its findings made articulate, has more than passing significance."[67] Following this line of thinking, African American elders' recollections about lynching and a culture of lynching challenge us to consider why, as retired Franklin Parish Louisiana public school educator Addie Bolton noted, "people are afraid to talk about those things even in the twenty-first century."[68] Bolton clarifies her remark and suggests, "There are still consequences that could follow your words. There are still consequences—many of them that we are not privy to—but you always know. So because people try to be extra-special careful, then they are reluctant to say too much about it."[69]

When I met with eight retired educators at Brown's Landing in Winnsboro, Louisiana, on August 13, 2009, fear emerged as a theme to describe why African American elders choose not to discuss lynching. A visit with Winnsboro resident Mrs. Anita McCohn prior to this gathering, an interview with Mr. Solon Marshall (who did not attend this dinner dialogue), as well as a review of news articles archived in Franklin Parish's only public library, and Michael J. Pfeifer's *The Roots of Rough Justice: Origins of American Lynching*[70] confirmed that at least one lynching occurred in this sector of northeast Louisiana.[71] In addition, Arthur F. Raper documents the

November 19, 1932, lynching of William House in Wisner, Louisiana, one of four hamlets located in Franklin Parish, approximately thirteen miles from Winnsboro, the parish seat. According to Raper, House, "accused of insulting (raping) two white women[,] was placed in the Franklin Parish jail and taken from officers en route to trial and hanged."[72] I listened as teachers who influenced my own social-cultural awareness and intellectual curiosity spoke forthrightly about a prevalence of fear associated with lynching. Of concern to me was my inability to connect their accounts and the emergent theme of fear-induced silence. As I recalled my elementary education, I had no recollection of discussions about lynching in Mrs. Bolton's Wisner Elementary School's fourth-grade social studies or Mrs. McCohn's Wisner-Gilbert Junior and Senior High School's seventh- and eighth-grade history classes. What this impromptu exercise confirmed was a manner in which history, and thus *education*, is often determined and transmitted via a predetermined sanitized curriculum as a way to silence truth.

With limited resources, these now retired educators taught in a segregated system for sixteen years following the Supreme Court's landmark decision in *Brown v. Board of Education of Topeka* in 1954. These educators drew on their faith and commitment to social uplift espoused by the black women's club movement[73] and African American Greek organizations.[74] These educators were not deterred by a superintendent's actions to end segregation with "all deliberate speed" that translated into diverting federal funds to found all-white *Christian* academies to the detriment of black and poor white public school children. For these retirees, knowledge was a strategy of choice to combat deeply entrenched poverty in this rural northeast Louisiana area. As such, their actions suggest that silence is not necessarily acquiescence to things as they are but rather a contextual response to preserve life.

When understood from this perspective, I can better appreciate strategies these and other black educators held in tension with cultural realities. Rather than succumb to fear, they embodied countercultural techniques—for instance, to (a) mentor students in academic subjects and the industrial arts; (b) develop relationships with parents, many whom could neither read nor write beyond a second-grade level, whose intellectually gifted children would become the first in their families to graduate from college; (c) provide scholarships and internships as an investment in students' potential; and (d) expose students to the arts.

A stroll through Winnsboro and windshield tours of Gilbert, Wisner, and Baskin reflect painfully results of African American migration as many students mentored by now retired educators chose not to return to this area. Blight is evident on almost every corner. Quality of education has declined with "Louisiana public-school students ranking 49th in the nation in academic achievement."[75] And, as Gilbert resident and retired Franklin Parish School administrator Mordessa Corbin commented, "The culture of fear still exists." For Corbin, this socio-national reality is "just the bottom line."[76] It is a culture of fear predicated on a fabricated dichotomy of blackness that is antithetical to an imagined whiteness. This culture of fear epitomizes a creative license to arbitrarily assign honorary status to other ethnic groups. It is this national pathology that perpetuates a fearful hesitancy that relegates discussions of lynching to kitchen tables instead of the public square.

Race and Violence:
"Not comfortable with the issue of race"

With the election of Barack Hussein Obama as the forty-fourth president of the United States of America, many were quick to proclaim the advent of a post-racial society. This declaration suggests a pseudo ideal that both disregards the uniqueness of humanity and ascribes a form of absolution that exempts certain persons and systems from past, present, and future acts of racialized violence. To imply that race does not matter exacerbates, as Mordessa Corbin explains, "the reluctance to talk about anything that is racial, because in your Deep South, and probably also in a lot of areas in your western states, those that border Canada like the Dakotas, you still have a lot of racial prejudice and you still have—the conversation on race is not an easy conversation for most people."[77] Fifty-plus years after "Bloody Sunday"[78] was televised around the world and days after the Department of Justice released its investigative findings on racist practices within the Ferguson, Missouri, Police Department,[79] difficult but necessary conversations occur all too infrequently.

Rather than name racism as a national sin, there is a greater tendency, as Corbin opined, to "sweep it under the rug than to talk about it."[80] Clearly, a recent onslaught of deaths of unarmed black persons at the hands of police and others[81] counter any claims that silence is an antidote to diffuse a neo-lynching culture. At the same time, we acknowledge, as does Corbin, that those who confront government-sanctioned practices of terror do so often at great personal and communal risk. Despite a national narrative of truth and justice for all, Corbin rightly notes that how we respond to race and violence has

a lot to do with the fear, and the fear is not necessarily a physical kind, even though that does exist to
a degree—you have a fear of retaliation by economic
means. The suppression is still there, and now, instead
of using the physical, we use the economic sweep and
it can be so effectively used on both white and black
until it just makes it uncomfortable. Plus, you never
know to whom you're talking, and so it makes for
reluctance in conversation. Also, I think it's really difficult to face that because in a sense, you feel a coward
because you don't face it. It's more comfortable to let
it slide, and that's what we do—we take the more comfortable route.[82]

We find ourselves increasingly confronted with racial issues
that are cloaked in ambiguous national jargon supported by
contextually informed interpretations and applications.

If racial profiling, excessive police force, and occupied
neighborhoods are indicators of the United States' moral
barometer, we are, as Corbin stated, "really in trouble as a
country until we can see how the racial divide is hurting our
growth."[83] For Corbin and others, the growth to which they
refer is not measured in terms of economic profit and loss.
Rather, growth is determined by an individual and collective ability to recognize and respect the full human dignity
of another person. It is a commitment to dismantle systems
designed specifically to "use violence to beget violence"[84] in a
manner that disrupts an often silenced narrative regarding
foundational practices traceable to this nation's initial occupation of this land.

Cultural Realities of a Shared National Narrative:
"A hard thing to accept"

Following a grand jury's December 2014 decision not to indict a police officer in the chokehold death of New York City resident Eric Garner, the hash tag #ICantBreathe populated social media sites. These final three words were uttered by Garner as he lay dying on the streets because he dared, after he informed police he was not selling loose cigarettes, to question a pattern of public harassment. In a climate where an assessment of *a threat of present danger* determines, in a growing number of incidents, the level of force to which black bodies are subjected, #ICantBreathe epitomizes the ineffectiveness of the law as an instrument of justice. #ICant-Breathe, a symbolic reminder of lynching and a culture of lynching, infuses new meaning regarding African American elders' decisions to discuss this horrific period. For many who lived during an era marked by the possibility that they and their communities would always be subject to a constant state of siege, retired army non-commissioned officer Martin O. Collins mentioned, "It's a hard thing to accept and back in that time they couldn't do anything about it." From Reconstruction to Jim Crow; from white sheets to police shields; from clubs, dogs, and water hoses to military tanks and tear gas; from Bull Connor in Alabama to Governor Jay Nixon in Missouri; from Philadelphia, Mississippi, to Ferguson, Missouri, lynching culture is a quasi-industrial complex from which a few benefit financially from extra-legal activity. #ICantBreathe is a rallying cry that connects African American elders' lynching narratives to on-the-ground documented accounts of legally sanctioned domestic terrorism in cities across the United States.

Born in Sicily Island, Louisiana, on March 9, 1932, Collins completed one semester of undergraduate study at Southern University in Baton Rouge, Louisiana, before he enlisted in the army. During his twenty-two-year military career, Collins was stationed in Hawaii, Kentucky, Louisiana, Oklahoma, Texas, and Virginia as well as Germany, Korea, and Vietnam. Familiar with military rules of engagement, Collins also recalls a time when the United States "had laws on the books but they didn't affect black people—they didn't protect black people." Tracing his earliest memory of lynching to approximately five years old, Collins describes the killing of a young man by police. Collins said:

> [I] heard people talking about it. . . . So this young man sold his cow and his mother, she got mad about it and she told the police there in Sicily Island that he had sold her cow, so the police arrested him. I understand that the police really didn't like him anyway and wanted to kill him, so he arrested the guy and he had a pickup truck. He told the guy to get on the back of the truck. He got on the back of the truck but he hauled off and shot him anyway and killed him.

Shot without access to due process of law, Collins acknowledges, "that was the way they did things." As he recalled another fatal shooting at the hands of a known person for failure to comply with a request, Collins said, "Now they worry about somebody killing their dog but back then they shot black people down like they were rabbits and put weights on them and put them in the river and all that kind of stuff. Everybody knows it—they did nothing about it. The laws didn't apply to them for doing black people that way."[85]

In the more than seventy-five years that bridge Collins' earliest memories of lynching and the Department of Justice's findings of police and judicial abuses in Ferguson that are a symptom of white supremacy, it is still hard for some US residents to acknowledge cultural realities of African Americans that transcend class and gender particularities. In spite of the fact that *crime* is itself a subjective notion, police "do not expend time or resources extensively policing"[86] neighborhoods populated by persons, for instance, who defrauded individuals through elaborate Ponzi schemes. Rather, some now argue that there is a fallacy to "convert correlation into causation: Black residents bear the brunt of police attention because they are black."[87] Until all crime, regardless of the weapon of choice, receives the same attention and deployment of resources, the killing of black bodies, disguised as public safety, minimizes any potential for a constructive national conversation and subsequent actions about race and violence.

Compelled to Remember: "We shouldn't forget"

Immersed in memories of lynching, African American elders give voice to present realities of life in the United States of America. African American elders baptized by waters that spewed from high-pressure fire hydrants during the 1960s civil rights movement have no difficulty understanding why #WeCantBreathe.[88] For these elders, forgetting lynching is not an option. A founding choir director and active participant in the civil rights movement, Nims Gay talks about lynching "to let them know that what you have gone through that you don't have to do it no more."[89] For Gay and others, like Mrs. Gwendolyn Brown Hill, it is important that current and future generations know multiple aspects of their history. Hill—sister of Willie Brown, the first African American mayor of San Francisco—voiced concern for persons younger than her who "don't really realize the effect of lynching—that it actually happened." Hill offers three reasons to substantiate this claim. First, she does not "think they can visualize that." Second, she "thinks the people who may have had generations of folk that did the lynching—I don't know whether they're embarrassed or whether they have grown up with a different attitude—I don't know, but I do know that they don't like to talk about it and we shy away from it and some people get angry." Finally, she suggested that a failure to talk about lynching is "more about denial than anything because nobody wants to admit that it happened."[90] Hill gives voice to shame and guilt that shrouds lynching and its ongoing residual effects.

It is essential, I believe, that individuals who remember lynching and a culture predicated on fear to control human behavior recognize that forgetting history is not synonymous with an unawareness of history that equates to gross miseducation. Perhaps this is why Philadelphia, Pennsylvania, resident Junius Nottingham Sr. said, on the one hand, "people don't like to talk about things that are hurtful, or things that would make them go back and dig up old bones." On the other hand, he realizes that "sometimes, like with these detective things, you've got to dig up old bones to get the facts." According to Nottingham, sometimes "you have to talk about things that has happened . . . you got to be realistic about things."[91] After all, as Mrs. Bozie Mae Walker stated, "We shouldn't forget, because that is how the heart and minds change."[92]

Because #WeCantBreathe, Reverend Wallace Hartsfield Sr., human rights activist and pastor emeritus of Metropolitan Missionary Baptist Church in Kansas City, Missouri, insists that talking about lynching can be cathartic. For him, talking is not optional. Hartsfield considers failure to discuss this evil dimension of the United States' heritage as "one of the reasons some of the people today don't even want to believe that that ever happened." Given that the United States markets itself as a model of democracy, it is not difficult to imagine a tendency by some citizens to advance a form of historical amnesia rather than acknowledge that "people could be that ruthless."[93] Yet this country's *red record* and its not exclusively *southern horrors and mob rule* cannot be denied. If black people are to breathe, African American elders who remember and share their recollections of a period marked by *strange fruit hanging from trees* remind us that the present is often a repetition of the past and a glimpse of that which is yet to come.

2

Courageous Truth Telling

Historical Remembrance as an Ethical-Theological Mandate

For many persons born between 1894 and 1938, to be black in the United States of America necessitated an ability to absorb pervasive life-negating cultural practices. Being born black in the land of the free and the home of the brave required that many individuals, who are now at least seventy-six years old, comply with societal dictates. To come of age in varied shades of blackness in the late nineteenth and early twentieth centuries symbolized to many African Americans who remember lynching that civility must always be informed by an analysis of this nation's complicated and tortured fascination with terror. Yet lynching and a culture of lynching in this country is a subject frequently associated with notions of culpability, self-reproach, remorsefulness, and humiliating disgrace, with conversations rarely designed to incorporate narratives of African Americans, particularly persons who do not have national name recognition, as a means by which to broaden this nation's historical record. While many may recognize and applaud Mamie Till Mobley's *courageous* act to have an open casket at her teenage son's funeral and, in so doing, to challenge the world to grapple with "lessons of the hour,"[1] there is still a reluctance by some African American elders to talk about lynching.

Perhaps we can attribute this silence to the fact that some African Americans are unable to determine what might be accomplished in sharing their memories of such horrific events. For example, Ms. Clara Jeffries declined in an interview with journalist Leonard Pitts Jr. to describe a lynching she witnessed in 1930. According to Pitts, Jeffries asked, "Why bring it up? It's not helping anything. People don't want to hear it."[2] Other African Americans, like senior relatives of a friend whom I contacted before I launched the oral history project that informs this book, feign any knowledge of lynching activity, even though they resided nearly seven decades in North Carolina. I am not baffled when African American elders choose not to talk about lynching. Though much can be gained from their historical recollection, their silence reminds me that the residual effects of lynching and a culture of lynching must be taken seriously.

Unlike the Jewish Holocaust, which has international recognition, lynching continues to be associated with shame and denial—shame embodied by one too many who lived under this regime of terror, and denial by one too many who refute evidence preserved on postcards and other visual depictions. Because of lingering, though often unacknowledged, residual effects, lynching memories, like slave narratives, offer a different lens through which to evaluate personal and communal values. As such, dialogues on and about lynching cannot and should not be ignored. Participants in my oral history project who reside(d) in various sectors of the United States add depth to existing historical, sociological, and theological contributions on this difficult topic. Retired educators, clergy, scientists, veterans, entrepreneurs, lawyers, and laborers discuss lynching because, for them, historical remembrance is a theological ethical mandate. Whether these individuals acquired the equivalent of a first-grade education or achieved the highest degree in their field, lynching narratives, when viewed as oral epistles, challenge me to reassess notions of courage and the sacred. Literally and metaphorically, African Americans who recall aborted lynchings and strategies of survival invite me to consider how their stories shaped and, still unfolding in the shadow of lynching trees,[3] influence what is accepted as truth.

Although blood or the threat of blood is etched forever in the recesses of many African Americans' minds who came of age in the United States during a period marked by lynching, their socio-historical recollections can function as points of entry. These oral histories can serve as entry points to provide the human community another frame of reference from which to examine diverse ways in which notions of civility frame narratives that offer insights about these individuals' human capacity to make a conscious decision to go into their interior archives and determine for themselves if, or how, they will give voice to a truth that reflects their lived reality.

Long before the horrific events that occurred in the United States on September 11, 2001,[4] most African Americans, with at least seven decades of life experience, had vivid memories, even if intentionally repressed, of domestic terror. These select comments from oral histories about African Americans' experience with lynching culture confirm that persons were

executed for any little thing . . . they saw but they could
not speak . . . you don't ever want to be caught in the
woods after dark . . . always had to be careful where
we go and what we say . . . it was always a fear of white
people that was instilled into us as children . . . it's like
a horror story that humanity can inflict such a thing
upon humanity . . . you knew that people were lynched
but you didn't know a name of a person . . . you could
pick up the Negro press and you could read about a
lynching almost every week that was taking place
somewhere in the South.[5]

While I will never know fully the effect of lynching, oral historical accounts can function as a basis from which to evaluate strategies of resistance and visions of justice from which
to construct an ethic of resilience. As I weigh benefits associated with an *excavation*[6] of truths embedded and embodied
in African Americans' minds and souls, it is imperative to
acknowledge that courage—civility in our age—is connected
intricately to notions of justice as persons look back to times
past and reflect on current situations as a mirror by which to
assess how truth telling might inform a national response to
a *war on terror.*

I contend that it is virtually impossible to think about
the contributions of African American elders, whose oral
narratives inform my notion of courageous truth telling,
without also recognizing that they, like their contemporar-
ies who elected not to verbalize their experiences with and
about lynching, probably recognize a correlation between
memory extraction and training in detecting and defusing
improvised explosive devices. It is this knowledge of immi-
nent danger that will, more than likely, inform an internal

assessment from which persons who live with a historical reality that contradicts notions of human civility determine whether or how their truth telling may further the common good. In this regard, courage is not an abstract trait. Rather, courage is a contextualized response informed by an understanding of self that seeks to actualize a prophetic mandate "to do justice, to love mercy, and to walk humbly with God" (Micah 6:8b). Thus, courage is a reasoned decision neither to advance a conspiracy of silence to promote miseducation nor to condone racial hatred. Quite the contrary, courage is a virtue that demands that we acknowledge that truth, a way of knowing that is intricately connected to our existential reality, when detonated—given voice and space—can have far-reaching consequences. Courage thus calculates costs associated with danger and imagines creative, safe, and liberating movements.

Human Agency and Cultural Astuteness: "Hurts me deep on the inside"

Whether memories of lynching and a culture of lynching are preserved for future generations is contingent on a number of factors. For some African Americans, documenting these narratives is an ethical mandate. Yet to ascribe normative status to this position devalues conscious decisions to remain silent, not as an act of cowardice or historical complicity but rather as an act of agency to preserve one's own sense of well-being. As a nonparticipant in Sumter, South Carolina, mentioned, consideration must be given to possible repercussions. After all, as this gentleman pointed out, to talk is also to live with possible consequences associated with sharing memories that could result in confronting a non-law-abiding past that is fraught with ambiguity and sentencing disparities. On the other hand, as one contributor stated, "When I talk about it now and I think about it, I really have a lot of anxiety about that."[7]

I cannot ignore these concerns. To do so would be tantamount to inviting African Americans who remember lynching to step on a land mine. As retired Oakland public school educator Leola Arnold suggested, persons may choose not to vocalize their memories of lynching

> because they may think that it will stir up something and cause some of the problems that we're having right now. Because, you know, every so often when people bring up various things that's happening now, and they'll say, "We don't want those days to come back." And maybe they think it might stir up some of the things that happened then. And people feel that, well, you know, it happened then, but it's not going to happen again—and that way of doing. Maybe that's it.[8]

I could make a good argument to support reasons why some persons choose not "to remember the hurt that you felt—the pain."[9] Though Pastor Clarence Kidd elected to share his memories of lynching culture, he also noted that he would prefer not "to even think about that. When I do now, I get angry—something like that happening. It hurts me deep on the inside to even think about it. Your fear your anger. I don't want to think about it—that sort of thing happening all over again."[10]

Whether these senior citizens share a dimension of their remembrances of lynching or not, each, at various levels, engage in a form of conscious memory exploration that denotes the power of human agency. In some regards, this intentional decision to examine and, in some instances, to reexamine what some "Remembering Lynching" participants describe as a life-defining moment requires an ability to navigate, with care, those deep interior places where memories are stored. Given the violent nature of lynching and a culture of lynching, as well as the age of persons who experienced the reality of domestic terror as an ever-present threat, to discuss this societal practice necessitates that any act of recall be coupled with deftness to know how to avoid detonating life-negating triggers associated with long-term suppression of traumatic events. Just as we will never know how many individuals died *at the hands of unknown persons*, African American lynching narratives remind me that we may also never know how many persons escaped an attempted lynching. Oral histories of African American elders reveal that some recount personal incidents of aborted lynchings,[11] while others describe strategies of escape negotiated on behalf of relatives, friends, and strangers.[12] For instance, Elder Willie Matthew Thomas of Birmingham, Alabama, described a series of events that occurred when he "was between eleven to twelve" with persons near Tuscaloosa, Alabama, who threatened to lynch him. While he waited for his uncle to pick him up, Thomas said,

> Here comes this white lady down the street. I'm on this side of the road and she's on that side. . . . And this lady come across—she came right side the street, the road—the road wasn't very wide. And she went to the little corner there and she went down the road that leads down where my grandfather lives. . . . And she passed by. I knew her. Her husband and my daddy worked together in the mine. After a while, I heard this noise—dogs barking. The fellow—course it's getting dark—they had one of these lanterns and they come up out there. I asked them, "What's going on?" These big

ole dogs. . . . They come on up—I didn't see no shotguns
or nothing. . . . But they had them big old sickles, what
you cut down bushes and grass. . . . When they got to
where I was, they said—I can't remember exactly cause
I'm excited—between six and eight of them—they said,
"Hey, boy what you doing out here?" . . . I said, "I'm
waiting on my uncle." "You lie," and they sicced the
dogs on me—those great big ole dogs. . . . They couldn't
make the dogs bite me. Then they said, "What you
doing out meddling these white women?" I said, "What
you talking about?" He said this lady said that I said,
"Come there." You know, I'm just a little boy, you know
what I am saying? Lord, have mercy. That's back in the
days when they were doing a lot of lynching. And so,
I said, "Honest." . . . He said, "We gone hang you." So,
they said, "No, you out here in the dark—sitting out
here meddling these white ladies." Oh, no, a little ole
boy—I told them who I was. I said, "My granddaddy—
y'all know my granddaddy lives right down the road
down there from y'all."

What Thomas' experience indicates is that respectability politics, a way of behaving designed to avoid encounters with
white supremacy, has little salvific significance. As far as
these men were concerned, Thomas was another black boy
alone on the side of a dark road who was a threat to the potential safety of white women. Thomas realized that the fact that
his relatives "didn't give no trouble" was not sufficient to guarantee his safety.

Taunted by this small mob of men, Thomas said, "They
didn't hit me but they kept on cussing at me."

One of them said, "Well, look, we gone hang him or
is we not?" Another one said, "Sure, we gone to hang
him." Well, he said, "Where's the rope?" One said, "I
got one. I brought one." And so he made up the noose
and when they got it made, he said, "Well, let me try
it on and see how it works." And they put it round
my neck and it was a grass rope—you know how it's
scratchy. I was in pain. And he pulled it, and go, "Aw,
it's gone work. It's gone work." . . . They said what, "You
see that big tree down there in that hollow? That would
be a good place to hang him." Okay, said, "Let's go."
Jerked me, dogs behind me wagging their tail. They're
pushing me right on across the road.

Thomas draws parallels between his trek to a lynching tree
and Jesus' journey to Calvary. He said:

They led me away to be crucified—to be hung. And all
of a sudden, a car came up the road. . . . The man saw
what was going on and he made a sudden stop. He ran
out there and said, "What's going on here?" They said,
"We go hang him." You know what they call us back in
those days, "Go hang a nigger." He said, "Nuh-uh, not
his boy." Say, "What you mean?" "You go hang him,
he ain't nothing but a child. You mean y'all go hang
him?" And he said, "Yeah." "What for? He out here
meddling white women." And so he asked me, "Willie
Matthew, what's going on" I knew that he knew the
family. He was the man that hauled their newspapers.
I started talking and they started cutting in. He said,
"I'm asking him. I'm not talking to you." And they
said, "We're go—we going to hang him. We don't care
what you say." He said, "No."

This intervention afforded Thomas an opportunity to share in greater detail information about his circumstances. He informed this man:

> [I was] waiting on my uncle to pick me up—and he knew about that because he lived on the corner not far from where it happened. . . . He said, "Nuh-uh, y'all ought to be ashamed." He said, "You're drunk." Then I said I know the lady. I said her husband and my daddy work in the coal mine together. . . . I mean it really got to me. And she was lying like that. . . . He said, "We gonna hang him. We're gonna hang him." And he said, "Tell you what. If you hang him, you got to hang me too." And he went to his truck—to his car—he had one of those Ford cars, little coupes—and got a pump shotgun out of it, comes back there, and I was crying. He said, "Don't cry. Don't cry, Willie Matthew, don't cry." He said, "I'm with you." He said, "You gonna turn this boy a loose. Y'all be ashamed of yourself." . . . He told those folks, he said, "Well, even if he wanted a white woman, he wouldn't want her." I mean, he's just telling truth. You know they wouldn't turn me a loose. . . . He was going to shoot 'em. He said, "A truck gone pick him up. We gone see if he's telling a lie." . . . But my uncle had an old truck. It would run sometimes and sometimes it wouldn't. That was one of the times it didn't want to run, you see. He had to do something to it to make it go. He said, "We ain't gonna leave until we see him get on that truck." Do you know they stood right there—he with the shotgun, they with the dogs—and finally the truck comes.

Thomas views the actions of this individual who stopped and inquired about the mob's actions as divine intervention. At a time when he could have been lynched based on supposition, Thomas' experience highlights why it is important to avoid simplistic constructions of good and evil. At the same time, there is no doubt that Thomas subscribes to a theological worldview that affirms a literal interpretation and application that allows for the possibility of human encounters with God (or the divine) in the natural realm. From his perspective, "that was nothing but Jesus at that moment, at that time that man happened, if he had been earlier or later, I would've been dead. They was fixing to give it to me, they were drunk and they wouldn't leave until that truck come and I got on it and they went their way."[13]

Thomas recounted, "[I] went home and told my father about it. I told my mama about it. They was worried to death." Thomas' estimated age at the time of his encounter with the mob dates this incident in 1930 or 1931, two years before six men lynched Dennis Cross in Tuscaloosa, Alabama, and before retaliatory killings in other Alabama counties in the wake of the Scottsboro Trial.[14] Thomas' parents realized their fears were not unwarranted when they received news that the mob intended to complete what they began earlier in the week. Thomas provided the following details about what transpired:

> The man my daddy worked for . . . we didn't know that he was with the Klan. . . . So he come out to the house and told my father, say look, "They're trying to come get Willie Matthew again." He said, "I'm trying to stop them." He said, "They ain't supposed to go against my orders." He just admitted now that he was one of them, you see. He was the Grand Cyclops.[15] Wasn't that something? You never know who you're working

for. But, anyways, that part was good news to us that he was trying to stop them, you see. He said, "Now, here's what you do." He said, "They're about drunk and they may come anyway but hide this boy. Better hide this boy." He said, "They may come in anyhow." My dad said, "Well, thank you, bossman," he said. "But," he said, "I got this Winchester here. They go eat bullets until they all run out." And he, you know what he had to do? He put me in a box—got a big old box—and carried it way out in a field—straw field. Put me way out there in that field and hid me out there so, you know, when they come, they wouldn't get me. But it just so happened that they never did show up.[16]

This act of human agency exhibited by Thomas' father is predicated on an ability to delve into, extract, and examine details associated with a specific aspect of lynching culture that is fraught with tension. Perhaps this is why, as Alice Walker stated so adamantly in *The Same River Twice: Honoring the Difficult*, most persons elect not to talk about lynching and its residual effect to control human behavior through a silencing of countercultural perspectives. Thus, whether individuals contribute to our nation's historical record or not, each, through a process of internal assessment, signals that courage and truth are not abstract ideas. Neither are these moral virtues grounded in notions of absolutism. Rather, "Remembering Lynching" narratives compel me to reflect upon lynching as a legitimate cultural production of domestic terror.[17] Given this historical reality, courage and truth cannot be comprehended fully without a further explication of the role and function of symbols—tools used strategically to intimidate and restrict activity.

From persons who engage in *thick*[18] interior explorations, I glean additional insights about processes employed to recall traumatic events in such a manner that they *do no harm to themselves or to others*. Also, when the very act of lynching and its primary weapon—the noose—are internalized to ensure a silencing of history, African Americans who came of age during this death-dealing era offer insights into moral discernment that afford me another point of reference from which to examine the impact of sustained invisible wounds. It also stands to reason that I can gain a greater appreciation for persons whose lived experiences are antithetical to historical revisionary accounts proposed by some elected officials and educators.[19] When employed as primary resources, these oral histories are further evidence that, regardless of religious orientation, there are strategies of resistance and visions of justice that emerged from a culture designed to thwart a sense of human dignity that is of immense significance in a global capitalist society. Life in the shadow of the noose is fraught with ambiguous tension. On the one hand, it is a reality complicated by traditions and compounded by a desire to give voice to practices that reflect the worst of human nature. On the other hand, this state of existence seeks to honor that which contributes to the well-being of all to be coparticipants in God's unfolding community.

Personal Choice and Survival Mechanisms:
"Remember today just like it was yesterday"

As they recall personal accounts and "stories that history books didn't talk about,"[20] African Americans who remember lynching share life-preserving insights on ways in which they navigated land mines designed to infuse them with hatred. This astute awareness, characterized by some as a process of personal healing, resulted in many choosing not to succumb to "built up hate"[21] but rather to "put that hate down."[22] Over time, they chose to engage in a de-internalization process that enabled them to name lynching as a by-product of racism that is nothing more than systemic sin cloaked in language that is used adroitly to produce a desired response. Or as Katherine Clark Fletcher mused about the manner in which lynching affected how she read the Bible, "[I] never thought in terms of—I don't think I ever thought in terms of God forsaking us. I don't know that it had too great an effect on me. I just saw people who were full of anger and hate."[23]

All too often, though, as in the case of lynching, contemporary events indicate people forget too quickly, or maybe never really knew, or maybe choose to ignore, why individuals employ certain behavioral techniques. After all, as Hannah White Allen opined, "Who wants to know how bad somebody was beat up and how they hung them in the tree or—and just left them there, and especially—so a lot of people don't want to hear about that. They don't even want to talk about it. . . . It's kind of sad and you don't want to remember that. You want to try to throw it out your mind, but it's true."[24] Given the destructive nature of lynching and its residual effects on the human soul, I examine African American lynching narratives and identify similarities between justifications for preemptive strikes and a culture of lynching.[25] The former, executed by George H. W. Bush's administration, used militarism to advance this country's interests and geopolitical hegemony.[26] The latter became an accepted way to control a formerly free labor pool to minimize disruption to modes of production that were essential to sustaining a concentration of wealth, often under the guise of protecting white female virtue. Examinations of lynching narratives may offer remarkable insight on strategies individuals employ to manage the lasting effects of improvised explosive devices (IEDs), land mines, and shock absorbers.[27] At the same time, these survival mechanisms also challenge personal assumptions about the nature of God and the essence of humanity. Examinations of theo-ontological suppositions inherently call forth questions about basic tenets of Christianity.

For African Americans who lived through and now live with memories of a culture characterized by lynching, to remember is to give voice in their own words about a time when they "lived in America, the land of the free, but yet":

> There was not freedom . . . there was a fear . . . that was the way they did things . . . the threat was great . . . you never knew when or where . . . everyone talked in hushed tones about it. . . . [I]t was just something that happened.[28]

At the same time, while "that was just the process back then,"[29] to think about lynching, regardless of whether a particular account is included in public records, is also to provide a glimpse into strategies that continue to inform an individual's sense of personhood. It is perhaps this willingness to examine that which characterizes the worst in human nature, while assessing simultaneously personal and communal responses, that continues to function as a guide when navigating mental-emotional-cultural embedded symbols that, if not handled properly, could cause catastrophic damage.

From persons who "remember today just like it was yesterday"[30] we receive nuggets of wisdom that call into question notions of a beloved community that are compromised when privilege, in its various manifestations, condones behavior by individuals who are "not bound by any of the rules that went on there."[31] In these narratives, accounts of courage embodied by people who, for example, though "still black in a small white town,"[32] compel us to become informed citizens. Otherwise, we may find ourselves ill prepared to identify and navigate camouflaged improvised explosive devices, disguised for instance as economic policies and sentencing guidelines that seek to disrupt our mental-emotional-cultural constructions that shape our notions of that which is ultimately just.

Contextualized Formation of Self and Neighbor: *"Black community was on lockdown"*

African American lynching narratives are not ex nihilo accounts. Rather, personal memories about a specific phenomenon are intricately woven aspects of individuals' lives that offer us a glimpse into cultural-social-religious-political dimensions of the United States' national narratives. Thus, these narratives are both personal and collective, given they are framed by a historical reality that is neither *a contextual* nor an episodic anomaly. Yet, at some level, these narratives signify that the proverbial maxim—treat others the way in which you want to be treated—continues ultimately to shift responsibility for life-affirming human interaction to persons who are targeted for systematic destruction. This stance can, and perhaps should, raise questions about behavioral patterns that are so intricately woven into the fiber of the United States' sense of entitlement that it allows one-too-many citizens to become anesthetized to practices that, if observed in other contexts, would be characterized as barbaric. Thus, to some extent, I could make a claim that to assess techniques employed by diasporic persons of African descent who live in the United States is to engage in a process by which we glean insight into ways in which a particular generation navigated *mob rule* and *southern* (albeit national) *horrors* that may challenge assumptions about spiritual development and faith formation.

Many oral history participants characterize their faith in God not as an elixir but as "the only source of protection and strength"[33] to "endure many of the wrongs that was and is being done to us."[34] Others believe that "God was able to bring us through all of this if we only had faith in God—because we didn't have any power. The other race of people had all the power and we had to depend on God to see us through all of this."[35] At the same time, some participants, such as Dr. Freddie Cudjoe, "couldn't see that it [lynching] had anything to do at all with my faith in God. I couldn't see anything to do with my hopes for the future. . . . I could not see any hope that white people would respect, nor be mindful of my feelings."[36] Yet, in an era when a culture of neo-lynching is pervasive on college, university, and seminary campuses, faith in a God who abides with persons who are willing to die in order to bring attention to injustices can function as a strategy to effect change.[37]

"Remembering Lynching" narratives point to a people's capacity to engage in contextual analysis and to construct alternative responses that lend themselves to a development of counterterror approaches with desired outcomes to raise consciousness levels as well as lower risks of personal-emotional-psychological danger to subsequent generations. This oral recounting also highlights a method by which we can come to terms with our own responses to violence and a personal awareness about the ways in which we confront and transform our own varied expressions and degrees of embodied hatred. This is no easy feat. After all, as some noted, because the "black community was on lockdown,"[38]

they "buried this hate and anger for a number of years"[39] only
to discover that, perhaps in spite of national xenophobic sen-
timents, their faith in God, coupled with a personal commitment to civic engagement and educating children and their
parents, enabled them to arrive at a point where "a heavy burden had been lifted . . . and they had let the hate go."[40] This
intentional act of reorientation is neither a denial of societal
realities nor a romanticizing of an imagined world. Rather,
it signals a determination not to be controlled by internalized rage against persons who choose to behave inhumanely.
Instead, a decision is made to redirect energy into areas that
can yield a positive difference.

Given that a sense of personhood is shaped, to some
extent, by diverse communities of accountability, this
intentional act of release can be tantamount to a process of
(re)birth. It is a deliberate move to determine what steps are
necessary to divest of culturally imposed forms of power that
often function to dictate self-perception. A necessary step in
this process that may minimize traumatic effects to a person's body-soul-psyche is to acknowledge and avail oneself of
resources that facilitate a shift from thinking that anyone is
"just at the mercy"[41] of lynching architects to a mindset that
challenges lynching culture in its varied manifestations. It
is important to note that this ontological shift demonstrates
that a faith-informed response to evil is not static. Rather,
it is grounded in and informed by a contextualized response
that refuses to view self and neighbor as universal abstract
concepts. In other words, individuals subjected to ongoing
forms of violence concretize their experiences. African American elders who remember lynching and a culture of lynching
offer a non-abstract accounting of a world they were simultaneously subjected to and objectified by. Participants in my

oral history project discuss techniques employed to minimize the extent of internal and external injury, which is frequently contingent upon an individual's awareness of contextual distinctions.

Interestingly, there are parallels between responses to earliest memories of lynching and Ida B. Wells' 1892 three-phase approach to counter lynching. While Wells emphasized economic boycott, migration, and documenting cultural proclivities, several "Remembering Lynching" oral history participants noted, for example, "education was the only way out,"[42] while others stressed a need to "get involved"[43] as they believed and hoped "change will come if we participate and try to help the change."[44] Like participants in social justice movements in this country that span the abolition of chattel slavery to the 1960s civil rights movement, African Americans who remember lynching also acknowledge "there were a lot of good people" even if "they were just not speaking out enough."[45]

In light of this reality, while fraught with ethical-theological tensions, this imagery of (re)birth is an invitation to revise or reject previously unquestioned values. To come of age in a culture of terror and yet to arrive at a point where self-abnegation is transformed to love of self such that it becomes a catalyst where we "let justice roll down like waters, and righteousness like an ever-flowing stream" (Amos 5:24 NRSV) is, in some regards, an embodied expression of atonement. This act of reinterpretation conveys the power of resurrection that emerges from and is informed not by a death penalty enactment but rather by the potency of words attributed to Jesus—*it is finished*—even as he hung on a cross.

While most "Remembering Lynching" oral history participants view Jesus' crucifixion as essential to their understanding of salvation, the potency of the words uttered on the cross posits that without bloodletting, whether a form of sanctioned or extralegal capital punishment, (re)birth can emerge from an awareness that actions that contribute to the common good of the least of these contain power to transform us and the world in which we live. It is this sense of connectedness that can diffuse that which *seeks to kill, to steal, to destroy* in a manner that neither ignores culturally embedded hatred nor idealizes our existential reality. Rather, to engage in a critical constructive contextual analysis is contingent on our ability to cultivate behaviors that enable us to devise and implement techniques with which to navigate systems, confident God will meet us in the very particularity of our situation.

Neo-Lynching Society: "There are still times . . ."

Closely connected to courageous truth telling is a commitment to preserve life—both one's own and that of subsequent generations. While one elder drew correlations between lynching and death by execution in the electric chair,[46] she—like others who shared their recollections of communities that were, in some regards, under siege—suggested that we should not be too quick to assume that mob rule is no longer operative in the United States. For, as retired attorney Donald Davis, a native of Oklahoma, recalled,

> We had a hill in Sapulpa, before Sapulpa started spreading out, it's called Sugar Loaf Hill. You know, we didn't know any better, . . . innocence is something. I mean it can really strip the meanness, it can strip the veneer away from the meanness and it can strip the meanness away from the nice—it's just innocence.

We use to ride our bicycles up the hill and see . . . who
would get to the top, you know, and everything. That
was where they use to lynch the black folks in Sapulpa.
Sugar Loaf Hill. That time it was in the center of the
hill, they even had the post up there that kept the
iron steel post up there that they use to lynch them
on. I went to school with a fella named R. C. Jones—
good football player—had an eye for white girls. And
worked as a bellman at one of the hotels at night, and
they took offense with his attitude, they beat him to
the nth of his life—and took him over there across the
tracks and kicked him out on the ground, and this was
as recently as 1940 something. It's the same attitude
that still exists.[47]

Davis' recollection of space and memory offers a helpful
insight into potential consequences associated with a des-
ignation of property as sacred. Furthermore, the notion of
public-owned sites as markers of death does not in itself
address sufficiently factors of power and privilege.

Concurring with Davis' assessment of race and consequences of life in a neo-lynching society, Reverend Wallace
Hartsfield Sr. elaborates further:

Well, when I think in terms of some of the activities
of the political situation. And to see what happens if
they listen to some of the legislators, those who run in
the Congress—both sides of the aisles whether it be the
House or the Senate. And to hear some of the talk that
they do it's almost like it's intellectual hate. It's hate
with a rationale. And they want you to believe it.[48]

Given that a majority of the oral histories were recorded
between June 2009 and May 2010, parallels between

participants' recollections of *mob rule* and public responses
to the forty-fourth president of the United States suggest that
lynching is a sin with which the church and society continue
to grapple. In this regard, Donald Davis noted the following
public response to President Obama:

> People call it backlash, there ain't no such thing. It's
> just that you are getting more hatred rising to the top,
> and filling us with the Tea Party people and the South-
> ern "Republicans," that's what they are, Dixie-crats,
> they are nothing but old warmed-over Dixie-crats. You
> are getting them fanning the coals and you are getting
> more blazing attitude among people. You are getting a
> lot of hatred out there now. People talking about how
> it was such a wonderful thing Obama—yes it was—but
> it is also a terrible thing in the sense that you are not
> going to put up with all of these real die-hard racists.
> But we'll put up with that. . . . I'd rather put up with
> that than not to have Obama. . . . Doesn't it scare you to
> see them walk to the rallies and the town hall meetings
> with their guns on their hips?[49]

A review of "Remembering Lynching" participants' vivid
responses to culturally embedded and present-day responses
to terror suggests, to borrow from Frederick Douglass' 1894
speech, there are *lessons of the hour*[50] that continue to merit
serious consideration. Of particular concern for many is how
a lack of knowledge of US history by a large percentage of a
post-1960s civil rights generation, particularly its black citizens, contributes to a reenactment of a culture of lynching
with persons ill-equipped to assess the import of cries to *take
back* a country perceived to be under siege.

Embedded in this hostage-like rhetoric is a disavowal of human rights that, at its most fundamental level, is predicated upon a perpetuation of mythological notions of privilege that often prohibit a forging of alliances across class lines. After all, some persons are so steeped in a false sense of racial entitlement that they choose to participate willingly in perpetuating stereotypical myths rather than engage in difficult but necessary dialogues from which actions to further a more just society might emerge. We need only to look at, for example, responses to George Zimmerman's July 2013 acquittal for the murder of Trayvon Martin. Only in the United States, as noted by several persons, could an African American teenager be tried and convicted for his own death at the hand of a white person or an individual granted honorary white status.

Then, as now, as Mrs. Shirley Johnson explained, lessons on how to avoid confrontation that might end in death were part of the fabric of black life. She recalled:

> [My family] had these conversations and I was raised up in an environment of fear and knowing that if you got out of line, you had to pay the consequences and my grandmother had told us when we started riding the bus, don't stop downtown, because you know if you go in those stores, if anything happens, they don't care who did it. If you're a black child in that store, they'll grab you. And I raised my boys the same way. I would tell them—don't. They didn't go to H. L. Green's when they got out of school. They had to come straight home, because I didn't want them—I raised them not to be victims, because that's the way we were raised. And we were raised in an environment where black people were victims, whether they were guilty or not.

With an astute awareness of current cultural realities, Mrs. Johnson spoke candidly about consequential similarities of being black during an epoch of lynching. She described in detail "driving while black" and emphasized:

> If you went beyond a certain area, you could get arrested just because you were in that area, because you were black. . . . And the saying that this is a free country—during this period of time, was not free for us. Just certain things that black people knew that they could not or should not do, certain areas they knew that they should not be caught in that area. And it was—well, it's still happening. There's no need of saying it was—it still is. There are still times when we are stopped, questioned about being in certain areas.

Here the complexity and ambiguity of freedom cannot be denied nor easily explained by biblical texts or hymns. A central tension is whether it is sufficient to encourage hope in a resurrected Christ in persons who are subjected constantly by a reality that signals that their ability to exist without fear may be little more than an illusion. Though she acknowledges some social changes, Johnson also admits:

> There's still a certain subtle racism, segregation, whatever you want to call it—bigotry that exists not only here in Dallas, but throughout the country. There are things that happen. . . . And the fact that bigotry and racism is still alive, it's alive big-time. And if you're black in the United States of America, if you haven't experienced it, you will. If you live long enough, you will, because it happens.[51]

A perusal of social media comments, articles, and interviews in the aftermath of the Zimmerman verdict[52] illustrates ways in which a particular event is often both defined and interpreted by personal and historical memory. Unfortunately, there is often a tendency among many persons in the United States to qualify experiences of non*white* persons that often unquestionably translates into furthering a construction of *whiteness* as normative, or the standard to which all others should ascribe. As a result, the lived realities of persons like Trayvon Martin and the many named and unnamed persons lynched in the United States suggest that a proclivity to romanticize, ignore, or caricature the intricacies of race as a determinant for what constitutes justice in this republic is to consciously or unconsciously sin.

Some might describe responses that ignore the insidious effects of racism embedded into legal policies, which can have a profound effect on current and future generations, as a form of *white privilege* accompanied by public displays of racial prejudice or even xenophobia. An examination of language and behavior across racial categorizations might point to a modern-day enactment of historical genocide informed by gross miseducation. Indeed, all we need to do is glance at illiteracy, incarceration, homelessness, unemployment, underemployment, and personal and national indebtedness statistics to know that at stake is a preservation of life. *By any means necessary*, it appears some are determined to maintain a preferred lifestyle to which they are accustomed, while others are driven by a desire to achieve "the" American dream, as others simply struggle to survive. Of ultimate concern, though, is what narrative(s) influence an understanding of humanity. At the same time, to name multiple shared narratives can be an invitation to participate in a collective process of truth telling in which space is created to hear, without a need to respond to another, and to engage simultaneously in a process of self-examination.

An Embodied Ethic of Veracity:
"Language of our memories is not an act to shame"

Notably absent from most constructive evaluations of lynching is a relationship between faith and African Americans' constructed responses to lynching, a domestic act of terror that rarely offered legal, not to mention moral, recourse. To address this, African American religious scholars, most notably James H. Cone, present compelling cases to emphasize symbolic correlations between "the cross and the lynching tree."[53] Rather than engage in an in-depth analysis of the crucifixion, this collection of oral histories necessitated an exploration between lynching and socially constructed and often interconnected intersections of race, gender, class, and other configurations that ultimately shape a person's and a community's ethic of veracity. For it is only when we, as Alice Walker asserts in *Living by the Word*, "hold up a light in order to see anything outside ourselves more clearly, that we illuminate ourselves."[54] There is connectivity in Walker's work that also fosters an interweaving of time past, present, and future. This way of seeing, being, and becoming challenges us, as Walker purports, to "understand we are who we are largely because of who we have been. And who we have been has come down to us as the vibration of souls we can know only through the sound and structure, the idiosyncrasies of speech."[55]

To concur with Walker is to acknowledge that it is often through a renewed appreciation of lived experiences that we can position ourselves to discover clues to facilitate our ability to name accurately that which represents the best in society as we articulate simultaneously that which denotes the vilest aspect of humanity. A primary objective is to discern how we can use our respective points of privilege to advance the common good. A complementary reason is to broaden ecumenical, interfaith, and national dialogues. This requires, or perhaps demands, that we, as Alice Walker encourages, reclaim our narratives. She says,

> It is because the language of our memories is suppressed that we tend to see our struggle to retain and respect our memories as unique. And of course our language is suppressed because it reveals our cultures, cultures at variance with what the dominant white, well-to-do culture perceives itself to be. To permit our language to be heard, and especially the words and speech of our old ones, is to expose the depths of the conflict between us and our oppressors and the centuries it has not at all silently raged.[56]

Or as Wallace Hartsfield Sr.—noted for his social justice advocacy at local, state, regional, national, and international levels—asserted in October 2007, "The language of our memories is not an act to shame." Rather, he insisted the "language of our memories is an act to illustrate hope." In this regard, truth telling requires that we give voice to ways in which justice has been misconstrued and misrepresented by architects of domestic terror whose sole purpose is to benefit from artificially constructed fragmentations.

Approximately five months before I defended my dissertation, which examined Ida B. Wells' three-phase approach to counter lynching in the late nineteenth and early twentieth centuries, I sat in the Kresge Chapel on the now former campus of Saint Paul School of Theology in Kansas City, Missouri.

On a Tuesday morning in October 2007, I sat and listened to the then seventy-eight-year-old Reverend Wallace Hartsfield Sr. articulate a personal desire to be in a more intimate relationship with Jesus. This statement piqued my curiosity. During lunch and a post-sermon community conversation, I asked Reverend Hartsfield to provide an illustration that would point to a defining moment in his life to which he might attribute his current spiritual state. In stark contrast to Walker's assertion[57] and Pitt's experience about a reluctance to discuss lynching, the current pastor emeritus of Metropolitan Missionary Baptist Church in Kansas City, Missouri, recalled vividly an incident that occurred in South Georgia when he was a young boy. Though Hartsfield did not use the term "lynching" to describe what happened in his neighborhood, his historical recall of a day etched in his memory suggests that truth telling is both a personal and a communal virtue that points to and heightens awareness about a specific phenomenon.

As difficult as it may be to imagine, Hartsfield's birth year, 1929, is viewed by some as the end of an era, 1882 to 1930, when "blacks were lynched in the South at the rate of nearly one a week."[58] In essence, African Americans lived in a terrorist nation replete with associated anxiety to avoid a confrontation that might result in a lynching. However, Hartsfield's earliest memory of lynching, which he described in greater detail during a July 31, 2009, conversation, suggests that while lynchings might not have been as prevalent, the practice itself was still a part of this country's landscape in 1937/1938. Hartsfield stated:

> [I] remember playing—in our front yard—a little
> town named Hazelridge, Georgia. We call it South

Georgia. I remember I was outside playing, and my great-grandmother who had been a slave—and I think she was—sixteen years of age, or seventeen, when freedom came—is the way they put it. I remember her coming out, and grabbing me by the hand, and told me, "Come in the house—come in the house." And I wondered why, because normally she would've just called me, and told me to come in the house, but she came out, and she—grabbed me by the hand, and—led me in the house, and I wondered what it was about, but she didn't say. And, of course, in those days, you didn't question, you know—the why of things. You just did. And so, being a boy, or whatever, I still wondered why, and so I was looking outside, through the—under the shade, as best I could—to see what was going on. Because the way she had had me to come in, had caused me to wonder when I was eight years old.

From an abrupt change in a primary care provider's interaction with a child to attentiveness to one's surroundings, black existence was often contingent on a proficiency to read—literally and figuratively—process, and interpret information that could mean the difference between death and life.

At the age of eight, Hartsfield did not grasp fully the import of his grandmother's action. As he continued to recount the events of that fateful day, he said,

I pulled back the curtain and looked out. And there was a pickup truck that came down the road. And there was some men—white men—in the pickup truck. And they was driving, somewhat slowly. And they was sitting on the truck, and—I think two or three—was in the cab of the truck, and a couple were sitting on the front, of the truck, outside, and a couple was standing—in those days they had running boards on the truck, and then were those sitting in the back of the truck. And there was something they were dragging behind them.

Hartsfield goes on to explain:

[I] didn't know what that was, until later I found out that it was the body of a black man, that had been—lynched. And, he had been, you know, hanged and all. But then, my understanding is that he had been taken down and then—well, before he was taken down—the body was used for target practice. And they were gonna shoot him, with guns and all. Then they dragged him through—in those days what they called Nigger Quarters—and that, I suppose that was supposed to be an example, you know, that would say to other black men, "This is what happens, to—" As in those days, they used to call us "uppity" Niggers because you—in those days, the white man didn't want a black man to look him straight in the eyes. Talk—he had to—talk with his head bowed. Kept him knowing that he was subservient—and I have later found out what, from what I could hear—was that the man worked for—a large landowner. And his wife worked for this man in the house. And that this man had been, taking, you know, advantage of his wife—with sexual advances, and that kind of thing. And he had just asked the man if he would not do his wife like that. And that was—the reason. And that's my understanding of what happened. I suppose that as a eight-year-old boy I just saw this going through the street—I didn't know what in the world was going on. But I knew something was dragging behind the truck, I didn't know what it was at the time because I'm inside the house. But that's what was said to me. And later, as I asked—questioned—they would—in those days, they wouldn't just tell you what happened. But it caught me so as an eight-year-old boy. I couldn't get it outta my mind, and I kept asking, you know, just kept asking—kept asking about, that.

Hartsfield's earliest memory of lynching illustrates that survival for many black people in the United States depended on an ability to read accurately cultural indicators. He and others who speak candidly about lynching do so, in most cases, out of a sense of urgency to convey to younger generations the validity of an axiom—*those who forget history are doomed to repeat it*. Yet, as Hartsfield explained, there are too many people who have no historical knowledge about anything related to lynching and are therefore unable to make appropriate historical-contemporary connections. As Hartsfield so aptly notes, we

> have to keep in mind that people who were born—after 1950—they have no idea, what you are talking about. And they're also shocked. Now, many of the people who were born, up to 1950, experienced segregation, but, it wasn't—it wasn't the rank, raw, rugged—segregation, because—what was it in '54, when the Supreme Court case—and all. Well, you see, a person who was born after '50, when the Supreme Court case came up, they were either three or four years old. So—they have no idea of what happened before that. And, even people who were born, let's say, in the middle '40s, didn't experience the—the rugged kind of thing. And even those who lived in large cities didn't have that kind of experience. It was the small towns and—those kinds of things. And when you talk about something like that,

it's hard for folk to believe that. That—that would even
happen. It just—it just shocked, and all. I don't know,
I get the feeling that some that have—that bother me
about talking about that. And for a long time, I didn't
even want to talk about it.

As a corrective to his broad generalization about a lack of
historical knowledge to lynching, Hartsfield distinguishes
between what he describes as "rank, raw, rugged segregation"
that characterized the United States prior to 1954.

It is interesting to note that his decision to discuss lynching was cathartic. According to Hartsfield, "It seems as
though that if I were gonna get any deliverance, I was gonna
have to—talk about that. As I've said to you, I was getting serious about my faith. I wanted some deliverance. I wanted to be
able to not hate folk." As he reflected on why he moved from
a posture of internalizing his memory of lynching and a culture of lynching to one of talking about this heinous act and
societal dysfunctionality, Hartsfield indicated that he arrived
at a point where

it was just such a burden, to carry that. And, it didn't
happen overnight. You know, the deliverance, but I'm
thankful at this time I can remember what happened,
and—but I don't hate white folk. I can talk with people. And I know that that happened, you know, and all.
And I—but I know that the persons I'm talking to—
they didn't do it. But—when I see the kinds—some of
the kinds of things that happen now, it's a reminder.

Reverend Hartsfield's conscious decision to talk about
lynching as a means of grace provides remarkable insight
about the necessity to preserve oral epistles whose theological

truths compel us to discuss candidly ways in which many defied culturally imposed odds as they fashioned a world for themselves and dared to imagine that things would be better for them and future generations. However, Hartsfield does not ignore pain associated with remembering. He admits:

> It still hurts. And people feel, well, by now, you ought to be over it. But, no, I don't think so. I don't have to be over it. I can remember it. But I don't have to remember it in hate. I can remember. But I don't have to remember in order to get back at somebody. My ministry now, my dear, is—that of clinging to hope.[59]

I find something much more profound at stake when I consider that "Remembering Lynching" oral histories are source documents that illustrate a depth of faith that enable persons, such as Hartsfield, to (a) name their reality on their own terms, (b) participate actively in their own rite of remembering as a spiritual discipline, and (c) find God, to borrow from Ntozake Shange, within themselves and love their God fiercely.

Ethical-Theological Mandate to Remember: "So that we don't return there"

Although the Tuskegee Institute's Lynching Inventory has, since 1882, compiled information related to lynchings that occurred during the years 1865 to 1961,[60] it, like other resources and sources on lynching, is incomplete. The award-winning work of selected scholars outside the theological academy, such as historians W. Fitzhugh Brundage's *Lynching in the New South* and Philip Dray's *At the Hands of Persons Unknown: The Lynching of Black America*,[61] provide crucial information that delineates lynching's direct effects on African Americans as well as the practice's indirect influence on the United States as a whole during the late nineteenth and early twentieth centuries. These seminal texts provide graphic and descriptive accounts of this country's infatuation with terror and document some of the extreme measures, to include ritual indoctrination of children to ensure a continuation of this legacy with brutality, employed to construct a culture of fear. Brundage's and Dray's research was not informed typically—like most publications on lynching,[62] though this is changing[63]—by narratives of African Americans who remember lynching.[64]

Even if trees no longer bear strange fruit,[65] a proliferation of stand-your-ground legislation in multiple states and racial disparities within the United States' incarceration system[66] suggests that black people remain in the shadow of the lynching tree. Individually and collectively we have a moral responsibility to respond in an informed manner so that we can fight injustice wherever it surfaces. Very much aware of a growing movement to erode human rights in the United States of America, Hartsfield, with more than five decades of pastoral experience, stresses that lynching should be a concern for the church in the twenty-first century for some of the following reasons:

> Number one—So that we don't return there—because we still have it, in various pockets, wherever you have people with the hoods, and those kinds of things. It is literally happening, as in the mind of a person, for it to happen.
>
> And then also, that the symbolism of lynching, that we need to deal with [it] in this twenty-first century,

it's the very symbol of lynching—which is injustice. It is the most hideous way of unjust treatment of not just the citizen—of a human being. In the twenty-first century, we need to be concerned about the symbol of injustice because it would declare that you're not human. There is no exception of personhood.

Because black folk, as you must have heard, at one point was declared they were not fully human. That was one of the reasons why the church was able to do what it did, in the days of slavery, and in the days of lynching, and all of that. The church, you know, it was not the prophetic church. It was the church that was caught up in the system, because for the church not to say that's wrong—is to agree with the system. And I think in this twenty-first century the faith community needs to deal with that, because the symbol of lynching . . . suggests that the church needs to be prophetic— even in the twenty-first century.[67]

Hartsfield insists that we must confront the horrific symbolism associated with a cultural practice of domestic terrorism that was often sanctioned, enforced, and executed by governmental officials if the church is to move from a place of accommodation to a prophetic agent in an increasingly globalized society.

For Hartsfield and countless others, a silent church is a complicit church. In its refusal to be a voice that proclaims consistently a word of truth, the church chooses, for various reasons, to condone injustice. In a world where slavery masquerades as human trafficking and where lynching is disguised as stand your ground, a historically and socially conscious church must engage in courageous truth telling. Because of this, conversations about lynching are designed not to foster popularity but to provide relevant information about cultural symbols and their embedded meanings. Even though symbols most commonly associated with lynching—the rope and bundled sticks that fueled human bonfires—are not displayed visibly, the church is called to remember that lynching functioned and continues to function as a metaphor to illicit a desired response.

When the church embraces and embodies its prophetic mandate to speak life, it does so fully aware that risks always accompany a decision to confront systems of injustice. In communities across the United States, individuals born in or before 1928 have a specific account of and about lynching that needs to be preserved. Some will remember persons whom they knew who died at the "hands of persons unknown." Others who survived an aborted lynching may reveal unlikely persons who aided in their rescue. There are others who will talk about lynching trees in their respective communities and discuss techniques they employed so as not to become paralyzed by fear of the unknown yet possible. With rare exception, African Americans who remember lynching offer remarkable insights about the human capacity to forgive without forgetting, to survive and even thrive in the midst of unimaginable evil. I draw upon the memories of these bearers of history as I purpose to embody that which is ultimately good. I have found renewed justification never to forget inhumane practices and strategies employed by many to counter a basic tenet of Christian faith: that all people are created in the image and likeness of God. In a context where social and theological perspectives of humanity were contradictory truths, it was crucial that African Americans knew how to excavate philosophical truths embedded in their lived reality. In direct opposition to prevailing customs, African

American elders who remember lynching benefited from a life-affirming interpretation of their sacred texts from which they sought to fashion traditions in the shadow of lynching trees, traditions that may one day enable all of us to divest ourselves of oppressive behaviors. If lynching narratives, like slave narratives, when told from the perspective of African Americans, provide another aspect about a shared existence in this country, the time to preserve these conversations is now. We cannot afford to wait.

3

Faithful Witness

Oral Narratives and Human Agency

Elders who entrusted an aspect of their memory about lynching and a culture of lynching to me represent black prophetic practices.[1] Each contributor has a story to tell about life in the United States that disrupts a carefully crafted version of civilization. Even if unconsciously aware of an association of power and rhetoric, oral history participants use language symbolically to describe how they understand themselves in relation to others. Their reflections convey an understanding of human dynamics that stand in tension with a basic Christian tenant that all people are created in God's image. Thus, to give voice to dimensions of race as a polarizing religious factor necessitates a reexamination of a universal concept of the *imago Dei*. Despite verbal declarations of love of God and all humanity, sociohistorical evidence suggests that encounters by African Americans with proponents of lynching and a culture of lynching provide accurate depictions of individuals' relationship with the divine. This realization of an embodied theology that situates expressions of God in diverse sites of worship, from beyond the confines of a church house to the foot of a lynching tree, contradicts notions of a palatable testimony. When it comes to lynching and a culture of lynching, we must ask ourselves whose account we will believe.[2]

In the black church, to testify[3] is to give a faithful accounting about what God has done and is doing in the life of a person or community of people. This focus on divine action is an expression of faith informed by a mandate to engage in a process of intergenerational transmission. An act of obedience not to be misconstrued with acquiescence, testifying, when perceived as a religious obligation, may necessitate that individuals learn how to respond in life-affirming ways to the psalmist's query on how to translate and transmit a realistic accounting of the human condition. When elders talk about lynching, they convey a powerful message that illustrates their adroitness to navigate within a country that is simultaneously home and alien. When black people testify about an experience of exile in a nation that self-promotes as the epitome of democracy, they signal to countless generations, now and to come, that Christians have a moral responsibility to learn how to "sing the songs of the Lord while in a foreign land"[4] where, increasingly, black life is expendable.

Black Lives Matter: "Not even human"

Any discussion about lynching should be intricately connected to practices of justice that critique and call into question US policies that reject the validity that black lives are of importance. As a personal and communal characteristic, justice is informed by repentance that emerges from and is informed by a manner in which one benefits directly or indirectly from systems. Furthermore, the notion of justice does not in itself absolve individuals from confronting complex legacies that complicate their own sense of identity. Justice demands an accounting for and a commitment to eradicate systems that ascribe nonhuman attributes to persons who are intentionally perceived as other. Given what we know about the historical operation of white supremacy in this country, projected animalistic characteristics upon black people continue to serve as a basis from which to justify killing, for instance, a twelve-year-old child playing in the park or a young man playing with a toy gun in a department store.[5]

Such observations underscore the relevance of a hermeneutic that recognizes depictions of blackness as antithetical to representations of life as a gift from God. Thus, I was not surprised that when asked how lynching shapes an understanding of justice, respondents drew correlations between their faith in God and pervasive racial profiling that is operative in an increasingly industrial police complex[6] described often as police militarization.[7] To accept this notion as a given assigns value to equipment without consideration for differences in mission, training, and rules-of-engagement. With a shift from protect and serve, police officers in the United States, unlike military personnel, can use military equipment without compliance to protocols established by the Geneva Conventions[8] to view African Americans as enemies of the state. This construction of blackness as something other than humans with rights is not a new phenomenon. At a time when the use of military equipment by police to manufacture a climate of fear is similar to tactics employed by plantation overseers during an era of chattel slavery and reinforced by "sundown laws"[9] during an age of Jim Crow, Mrs. Lois-Louise

Miller opined that "if you're on one side you get just, on the other side you get ice."[10]

Like Miller, Junius Nottingham Sr. maintains there is "an unevenness in the justice system." For this reason, he does not "have that much faith in justice."[11] While Mrs. Katherine Clark Fletcher "hoped for justice,"[12] Mrs. Sarah L. Hardimon remarked that she is "very skeptical of our justice system today."[13] Media accounts of black lives killed during encounters with police, contrasted against images of white killers taken into custody,[14] suggest that "hands up, don't shoot"[15] is a rallying cry that connects African American elders' lynching narratives to on-the-ground documented accounts of legally sanctioned domestic terrorism in the United States in the twenty-first century. As they remembered a climate that allowed for unchecked brutalization against black people, some elders noted they "don't think it was justice at all,"[16] while others declared, "justice now is still not the way it's supposed to be."[17] When asked how lynching shaped his understanding of justice, Collier Parks Jr.—a native of Benton, Louisiana, born November 17, 1933—recalls that, like his grandparents, he remembers "there wasn't any justice for black people."[18] The November 28, 1912, lynching of Wood Burke, James Heard, and Silas Jimmerson, and the January 26, 1918, lynching of Jim Hudson in Benton, Louisiana,[19] support this claim.

By the time Parks was thirteen years old, Bossier Parish, with Benton as its parish seat, had thirty-one documented lynchings. And between 1878 and 1946, the bordering parish of Caddo had twenty-seven documented lynchings.[20] According to Parks,

Whatever the white man did and said, that was it regardless—he didn't have no regard—nothing but his justice and his justice was, if you didn't do what he said, he took the law in his hands. He was the law and he done what he wanted to do. There just wasn't any fairness in the law. I mean the law was probably there but the white man executed it like he wanted to execute it—whatever he done to other. Klansman backed him up. He could come down and whoop a black man almost to death—sometimes he did whip him to death. Wasn't nothing said. There just wasn't too much justice for us. I don't guess we was even considered citizens. We weren't even considered human.[21]

To be recognized as something other than human could, as Solon Marshall remarked, cause some to "wonder if there was a God."[22] On the other hand, this construction of otherness by architects of terror caused Reverend Zan Holmes "to struggle."[23] A retired elder of the United Methodist Church, Holmes explains that lynching caused him to

struggle with why and how do I explain that in terms of faith. And to some extent to see Jesus on the other hand, as one who was crucified unjustly, see him as one who identifies—can identify with that rate of the lynching. And to—the injustices of that, of his death and to see that at the center of our faith, that death, that crucifixion, as the center of our faith and to see the resurrection as a way of life coming out of that—victory coming out of that or to put it this way, to just understand how one can be a good steward of one's suffering for the sake of a brand new future.

Holmes has an astute awareness of race relations in the United States. Sensitive to theological stances that dismiss contemporary realities of persons who live with a present threat of danger in this country, Holmes explains that while his personal concept of stewardship in relation to human suffering is beneficial to him,

> it continues to be a struggle. Because how do we preach to people who are still going through that kind of stuff? And every day, how do we preach to them? How do we give them hope? And you know, I have struggled within my faith. It enables me and it gives me hope that we can live in spite of that. And we serve a God who identifies with pressure and who gives us the power to overcome that. But it's still painful.[24]

While there is hope that life in this country is "not going to always be the way it is now,"[25] political rhetoric suggests that this nation has not gleaned insights from practices, like lynching, that rendered black people "not even human."[26]

Nation within a Nation: "In the dark of night"

Sarah Lee Robinson Hardimon grew up approximately fifteen miles north of Oklahoma City, Oklahoma, on a 160-acre farm in Arcadia, Oklahoma, that her family acquired (but no longer owns) during the Oklahoma Land Run.[27] Married to her high school sweetheart for more than fifty-five years, Hardimon describes her parents as protective. Hardimon's mother, Mrs. Bertha Elizabeth Robinson, ninety-seven years old at the time of my conversation with her daughter, was born six years after Oklahoma's 1907 statehood. Hardimon's mother grew up near Tulsa, Oklahoma, when "lynching entered a more racist phase."[28]

Although her mother was "about twelve years of age"[29] at the time of the Tulsa race riot and had personal knowledge of mob rule, Hardimon says, "[Lynching] wasn't something that they openly talked about because my father was a believer that—he didn't want to do anything that would diminish his children's self-esteem or make them fearful of anything, and so that wasn't something they openly talked about in front of us." At the same time, this protective stance was not synonymous with denial. As Hardimon recalled, "If we asked them questions about it [lynching], they would be truthful—not expand on any information, but anything that was negative about—well, Negroes, that's what we were called then—they would do that." From these descriptive accounts emerged a concept, even if not articulated explicitly, of a nation within a nation.

This concept of coexisting realities is an anathema that demands national repentance. A nation within a nation is an abomination that demands a turning away from idolatry constructed as patriotism. Thus, to repent is to turn away from objects of worship that function as sources of cheap grace that at their core undermine all of humanity. As Hardimon recalls the stories she overheard as a child, she remembers the "men particularly, farmers who shared information with each other, talking about the horrendous effect of their forefathers and people who had actually, maybe, experienced that [lynching] or witnessed it. I don't know if any of them did directly, but many of them came from places like Mississippi, Tennessee."[30] From these men, Hardimon received a civics lesson that may be essential in an evaluation of the role and purpose of school resource officers: "the permanent assignment of police officers to schools as a means of providing for the safety and welfare of students, faculty, and staff."[31] Just

as a high school teenager could be flipped from her desk and
dragged across a classroom floor, Hardimon remembers how
black men in Arcadia, Oklahoma,

> talked about some people coming into your house at
> night and just dragging you out and, you know, no
> questions asked. And they just really felt like they
> had no protection or whatever, because the sheriffs,
> the deputies or whatever—if somebody accused you of
> doing something, you was just at their mercy.

Exempt from due process of law in a land where freedom
to be treated with equality was little more than an illusion,
Hardimon's principal used historical narrative to supplement
a state-sanctioned curriculum. In so doing, he problematized
notions of democracy, justice, and fairness for his students.
As Hardimon noted, her principal "talked about people disap-
pearing, and maybe their loved ones would find them the next
morning hung up in a tree with a rope around their neck or
something, saying to black men, young men especially, about
that happening—could very well happen to them." These
instructions are still pertinent to black people in the United
States in 2016. These life directives are evidence that steps
must be taken to dismantle a bimodal form of nationhood.
Otherwise, persons subjected to neo-lynching will continue
to be denied justice in a manner that parallels Hardimon's
recollections of lynching.

When asked to discuss how lynching shaped her understanding of justice, Hardimon said:

> First of all, I felt that the people who were subjected to
> that had no justice. They had no protection from law
> enforcement that was supposed to protect all of the

people under their jurisdiction. And so, for the people who was subjugated to that, there was no justice. And nobody seemed to care that there was no justice for that segment of the people. There were people who cloaked themselves to be respectable people by day—judges, ministers, store keepers, some of the very farmers that these people broke their backs working for. And to the community, they presented themselves as these upstanding men—white men. But by night, in the dark of night, they were Ku Klux Klan, they were vigilantes, they were people who roamed in the countryside.[32]

Hardimon's description of a correlation between lynching and justice can function as a foundational principle for prophetic witnessing in the twenty-first century. As police killings surpass the worst years of lynching,[33] Hardimon's account invites us to name those spaces and places where persons with sanctioned authority are free to abuse power with minimum regard for accountability. Her recounting of things done in the dark challenge us to rethink a theological contrasting that privileges light as a penetrating source that pierces through, reveals, and eradicates evil.

Hardimon came of age when there "wasn't any fairness in the law."[34] She asserts that each generation has a responsibility to confront systemic injustice. To persons committed to the work of justice in a nation fraught with disparities, she says that

the torch is passed to you and you dare not let it die, nor you dare not forget the shoulders on whom you stand. . . . We are to always be open-minded, to always seek justice for all of the people, especially when we see injustice being perpetrated—for instance, the school bully. When you see someone bullying somebody else and you know that's not right, then you should step in in a way, to try to bring peace instead of making sport out of it. And so I would say to the young people that we need to always remember that we're all in this boat together and that we can go much further if we row in the same direction.[35]

Months before her seventy-sixth birthday, Hardimon understood that the election of a black president in the United States did not reverse automatically a "dual set of laws"[36] that guaranteed "no rights or no freedom"[37] would be actualized by a majority of persons of African descent. Because of this, she is adamant that our silence will not save us. At the same time, to work collaboratively to demand justice in a neo-lynching culture is to prepare to be killed at any time by forces and principalities camouflaged as purveyors of peace. Persons who engage in an embodied commitment to work on behalf of individuals and communities that live in near perpetual darkness do so out of a deep awareness and hope that life in this realm can be characterized by fairness, equity, and justice.

Reality of Black Life and Domestic Terrorism: "I couldn't love my country"

Mrs. Katherine Louise Clark Fletcher, orphaned at nine years old, relocated from the Denver, Colorado, area when she was ten and a half years old. The now deceased retired educator and public school administrator lived in Saint Joseph, Missouri, with her adoptive parents until she completed high school. The eastern terminus of the Pony Express in the mid-nineteenth century and the county seat of Buchanan County,

Saint Joseph is the sixth-largest city in Missouri.[38] Prior to
my visit with Mrs. Fletcher, she noted on her participant contact form that she had a classmate who was lynched in Saint
Joseph. She recalled vividly a lynching that took place "the
first year" she lived there. During an era when it was not customary for children to "question your parents," Fletcher discovered after she arrived home from a "girl reserve meeting
at the YWCA" that her "mother called to tell them there was
trouble downtown, to send all of the girls home and anyone
who had to come that way, past the courthouse, to give them
bus or streetcar fare so they wouldn't have to walk." Fletcher
provided information to contextualize her recounting of
events. With empathy for "the first child she had ever seen
who could not read," Fletcher explained,

> There was a young woman who supposedly had gone to
> a movie downtown. She lived on one of the main streets
> where she had access to the streetcar. . . . According
> to her, when she came home from the movie, she was
> attacked by two boys. Of course, she said that they were
> both Negroes. She wasn't raped; she just said that she
> was attacked. She was late getting home. But when she
> tells where this attack took place, she said a shortcut
> through an alley. But the alley was really out of the way
> for her to have been there. It was generally accepted
> in the black community that she was just making up a
> story because she was late getting home.

Although rape of white women was a key justification some
used to condone lynching, Fletcher's remark about this
particular individual does not necessarily signal her agree-
ment with an aspect of white supremacist culture. Fletcher
further noted:

These two boys were school dropouts, so they picked them up and put them in jail. No questioning, just "You two, you're in trouble." And they had been involved in some petty thievery, that kind of thing. The next day, some local people began gathering at the jail, men. By that evening, quite a group of people had gathered at the jail. Things were going fairly well until some of the farmers from outside of Saint Joseph and from Kansas came over. This is when the trouble started. A black lawyer in town got in touch with the governor to tell him he expected trouble and asked for help. We think that the governor perhaps didn't think it was that serious and delayed sending in help.

While intervention may not have resulted in a different outcome, delayed governmental action highlights a historical tendency to devalue black bodies as dispensable commodities. As Fletcher explains, the mob

> asked the sheriff for Lloyd—or for that—didn't have a name for the man. At first, he refused to give them anyone, 'til they threatened to break the door down. Now one account says that they did, but according to those who seem to know those who lived in the city, the door wasn't broken. But the threat was great because they had gotten a big beam to knock the door down. So the sheriff went down and he just decided—these two boys, he decided Lloyd and took him up and handed him to the mob.

This human transaction suggests that love of neighbor, as a Christian principle, should compel us to evaluate undisclosed assumptions upon which our actions are predicated. In addition, this exchange of black flesh requires that we first name accurately whom we disavow as neighbor and how this very delineation may offer significant insight about religious convictions. A mandate to treat others as we wish to be treated is often little more than a mythical mental configuration void of any correlation to reality. As Fletcher recounts,

> According to one person, Lloyd was stabbed in the back soon after he came up. I'm hoping this is what happened to him because they chained him to the back of a car and after brutalizing him some there at the jail, and then dragged him through the black community, the streets in the black community, calling him all kinds of obscene things.

Death by stabbing and dragging proved to be insufficient grounds upon which to atone for an alleged attack upon a young woman. To complete this public ritual, Fletcher said the mob "took him back to the jail, and by this time, I rather think he may have been dead. The general idea was that he was dead by this time. They hanged him to the tree on the courthouse lawn . . . and . . . built a fire under his body. We think that he was dead, and I hope to God that he was dead."

In high school[39] when this lynching occurred, Fletcher stated, "[This lynching on the town square] affected me in a horrible way. I was so full of anger and hate. Oh, I hated—I had to get out that day to go someplace. I hated every white face I saw. Oh, I was so full of anger and hate." Fletcher was angry at a system that induced a state of paralytic fear in her adoptive parents:

> [When I] got home, of course, the dragging of his body and all had taken place. My parents were in our house with the shades drawn and the lights out. My mother

was from Texas; my father was from Alabama. This is
the first time I had seen terror in their faces. . . . I didn't
think at that time, "Hey, they've come from a part of
the country where this is rather commonplace and
they know how serious this can be."

Using a strategy of resistance to minimize mob brutality similar to that employed by Reverend Wallace Hartsfield's grandmother, Fletcher and her parents "sat there in the house with
the lights out and the shades drawn the rest of the night,
really." While this was perhaps Fletcher's initial encounter
with the reality of how to navigate and negotiate domestic terrorism in the United States, she was unable to comprehend
fully her parents' and other community adults' response to
this tragedy. Consequently, she did not question a system that
elicited such a reaction from her; instead, she said,

[I] was more angry and disappointed in the—we were
called Negroes then. I was more disappointed in
Negroes than I was in the whites because in my child-
ish way, I thought they should stand up and make a
big fuss about it. In later years, I realized that most
of the people in Saint Joseph had recently come from
the South. This kind of thing—there was fear. It was
fear. So this is excusable, but I had to grow up before I
could realize it.

Eventually she recognized that her parents and others were
not in a position to change systems when "the police are in on
it. They're part of the lynch mob." However, before she experienced a cathartic process that allowed her to release internalized hatred, Fletcher had another encounter with lynching
within two years of Lloyd Warner's lynching.[40] Approximately

fifty miles from Saint Joseph, Raymond Gunn was lynched in Maryville, Missouri, for allegedly murdering "a white teacher of a small county school . . . who was found dead in the woods." When this occurred, Fletcher says,

> [I] was visiting my aunt where my sister lived. In fact I was to spend the night. I remember it was just dark, and a knock came at the front door. This is very unusual at my aunt's house. She stepped outside. Pretty soon the house just seemed like it was just full of people. A doctor, knowing that she had some extra room, had brought this family, the Gunn family, the relatives of the man who was lynched, had fled the city, Maryville, and had come to Saint Joseph and had no place. This doctor had brought them to my aunt's house. So all of these people were inside the house. They had, I remember, two small children. I was thirteen;[41] my sister would have been eleven at that time. . . . They just kind of turn the children over to . . . us to do something with, keep them occupied. I couldn't get any kind of reaction from the children. I realized now they were in shock. I didn't know at that time. And back in those days, grownups didn't tell you all the facts about things because talking could get you into a lot of trouble around the wrong people. We knew about the lynching; we knew they were there because they fled the city. But that's all we knew. I remember we put these two kids in bed with us. They're still not talking. . . . And there were people all over the house; on the floor, down in the basement, every place. When my sister and I woke up the next morning they were all gone.

While both Lloyd's and Gunn's lynchings were public spectacles, Fletcher viewed Gunn's death as "more horrific."

Fletcher bases her assessment on what followed after the ritual of lynching. She was appalled by the fact that "when the embers cooled, there were mothers with small children poking through the rubble looking for bones as souvenirs. I thought, 'What kind of human being is this, who could want souvenirs of—with children?'" Sadly, this is not an anomaly. Photographs of lynching provide historical evidence that children gathered around these sites of grotesque displays of barbarism. At these settings of horror, theology signifies what is central to persons who devote their lives to preserve culture as an act of religious fidelity.

Fletcher recalled a public display of national pride she observed in Omaha, Nebraska. About this event in which "all the schools were involved," Fletcher shared, "[I] walked along thinking to myself, I wonder how it feels to love your country that much because I couldn't love my country." Now, as then, Fletcher raises a valid question: "How can I love a country as much as these people do, with people who treat me the way they do?"[42] A theology that disregards black life is not informed by a tradition premised on love of God and neighbor. When actions suggest that black life is expendable, persons who self-identify as Christians must evaluate how their silence functions as a scapegoat whereby they avoid engaging in a process of self-examination that will inform repentance as a precursor to reconciliation.

Place and Space: "Everybody couldn't go north"

Even now, in response to Deacon James Drakeford's visceral reaction to his experience growing up in a culture of lynching, I remember my discomfort and a jolting recognition that I needed to shift into what I describe as a detached quasi-disembodied mode of engagement, which is antithetical to womanist sensibilities (except when separation is necessary to sustain one's own life), in order to hear and be present fully during interviews. The second oldest of eight children, Drakeford was born August 27, 1918, in the small town of Westville, South Carolina, in Kershaw County. The son of farmers, Drakeford "worked on the farm"[43] in a county created in 1791 that "developed its local economy through plantation agriculture, an enterprise dependent on African slave labor."[44] Tracing back his earliest memory of lynching to "about six or seven years old," Drakeford said, "[My] parents always told us, 'Don't say nothing to the white people, white women. Don't say nothing to them because they could have you lynched just by the word of mouth that she say you raped her.'" While this strategy of resistance might appear to be rather uncomplicated to deploy, it often required persons to rethink purpose and function of place and space. In Drakeford's case, for instance, he grew up in an area where "whites lived in neighborhoods side by us, side by side. . . . But they still would call you a nigger." With little recourse, Drakeford and others who came of age with a present threat of danger learned to deflect pejorative connotations of their personhood.

This ability not to internalize a worldview contingent on systematic dehumanization at all levels of society caused Drakeford to talk at length about persons he described as "old Toms"[45] who entered into black sacred spaces as infiltrators to "carry that message back to the white man." Appalled by this behavior, Drakeford bemoaned the fact that he did not "know why it was that a way but we hurt ourselves so many ways." At the same time, without acknowledging this experience of communal betrayal may have been a form of survival, Drakeford said that, regardless of individual accomplishments and legislative acts, black people in the United States are "still slaves. So we have nothing to celebrate. . . . Because we're still in some kind of slavery condition."[46]

This intentionality to name accurately conditions that seek to keep black places and spaces literally and metaphorically in a perpetual state of activity raises concerns about a theology of liberation when it appears that God is silent. Living between now and not yet requires an ability to imagine what a divine occupation in places and spaces that may remain unaltered during multiple generations may require of me. It is a good thing, according to Drakeford, to believe that "God will rescue us" from situations that are best characterized as hell on earth. Neither wavering in his faith nor minimizing conditions that shaped his sense of personhood, Drakeford reminds me that migration was not then and is not now an option for everyone.

In response to lynching as a societal practice that informed his sense of justice, Drakeford reminds me that while "we didn't like it; we didn't like it but what could we do? Everybody couldn't go north. We had to stay right down South where we were and hope that God will deliver us one day."[47] Southern states continue to bear the weight of this country's horrible legacy of race relations. Current accounts of racial tension in the United States are evidence enough to refute this myth. In every geographical sector of this country, African American elders who remember lynching extend to me a hope-filled message that compels me to consider ways in which my presence can transform places and spaces. These elders remind me that sometimes the only thing I can do is to remain where I am and link arms with someone else to counter forces of evil with a prophetic declaration that *we shall not be moved.*

Strength to Endure: "Only thing we had"

A resident of Oakland, California, for more than fifty years, Mrs. Rosalie Hilliard Joseph was born June 6, 1918, in Shreveport, Louisiana. A graduate of Central Colored High School, "the only high school for Shreveport's black population,"[48] Joseph recounts the manner in which her parents instructed her on how "to avoid contact with the whites."[49] According to Joseph,

> They didn't want me to have to come in contact . . . have no kind of friction with the whites. They trained me— well, I might as well say, they did it in the faith to be obedient to the white man—and his purposes and . . . how to avoid let's see—how to avoid upsetting him . . . how to stay put. In other words, the point of [it] is as I had heard, and . . . after I grew up, "Nigger stay in your place."

As the youngest of her parents' children, Joseph recalls an encounter between her fourteen-year-old brother and a white man on a public street when she was "about three or four" that serves to clarify parental instructions on knowing and staying in *one's place*. Joseph described her brother as "high strung" but did not have specific details about an exchange that happened while he was babysitting that "caused this man to slap him." What she does remember is that in response to this physical altercation, her brother "just pushed the baby, threw the baby out of the buggy, took the buggy, and whacked him [the man] across the head with it." Although Joseph does not elaborate upon this act of human agency, her characterization of what transpired next suggests that her brother understood the social implications of his actions.

While Drakeford is correct that "everybody couldn't go north," to remain in a specific locale was to resolve oneself to live with consequences grounded in principles of inequity and inequality. If I interpret Joseph's parents' guidelines on how to navigate spaces as a strategy by which to ensure their children were adept at how to circumvent danger, I do not question why her brother "started to run." Said Joseph:

> He came to tell my daddy. When he told my father about it, my father took him, he said, "Come on we gonna have to run now. You gonna have to get out of here." So he took him and carried him to the railroad track—I can remember that. And carried him into the railroad track and pointed him to that train, and told him, "You take that train and go north." And he took that train, and he went north. And I didn't see him no more until I was fourteen years old.

Joseph continued, "[At the age of three, I] heard my aunts and all talk about this, cause my mother couldn't stand to hear, to be mentioned that they took the blood hounds out and behind him to try to catch him. And they followed him, scented him until he got on the train, and then they couldn't scent him no more." This is, Joseph lamented, "the only thing I remember concerning that desperate thing in my family." With quick action, her family averted a close encounter with lynching. Or, as Joseph explained, "that was a form of lynching, they just didn't catch him and kill him." Exiled from home for approximately eleven years, Galberst Hilliard returned only after he confirmed that the man whom he hit was dead.

As Joseph reflected on correlations between lynching and justice, her ability to name lynching as "a part of white society" points clearly to a concept of a nation within a nation.

Her clarity about this aspect of ascribed prescriptive norma-
tivity shaped her religious worldview. For Joseph, coming of
age in a time when "there was a dividing line between the
blacks and the whites that's automatically known," she concluded that faith in God "was the only thing we had." Faith,
for Joseph, is not a passive enterprise. She recognizes that her
family's experience with a lynch mob "wasn't justice." Then as
now, justice is something for which we have to "fight"[50] with a
strong conviction that our faith will sustain us.

Beyond an Exodus Experience:
"Had to walk past that hangman's tree"

When I arrived at New Zion Christian Methodist Episcopal
Church (CME) in Benton, Louisiana, before dusk on Tuesday,
August 18, 2009, Pastor Clarence Walker Kidd and his wife,
Mrs. Emma Atkins Kidd, along with their grandson Samuel
Bailey Jr., Reverend Kidd's sister, Mrs. Margie Kidd Campbell,
and their childhood friend Mr. Collier Parks Jr. invited me to
take a short field trip. As we retraced a portion of the route I
had just traveled, I began to question a tendency to admire
landscape for its aesthetic attributes—miles of waterways
surrounded by natural foliage that by its sheer beauty evokes
a sense of calm—while giving minimum to no thought about
physical place and space and the stories contained therein. I
listened intently to these elders describe an account of geographical reconstruction that transformed and camouflaged
space from a lynching ground to an upper-income human-
made waterfront community. When we stopped on the bridge,
three of the elders pointed to an area in the center of the lake
that now engulfs a *hanging tree* that is forever etched in Clarence Kidd's, Margie Campbell's, and Collier Parks' memories.
From the interior of Pastor Kidd's minivan, I peered out the

window and realized that I was granted a rare moment to pay homage to unknown ancestors whose encounter with water offers revelations about matters of life and death.

This informative field trip elicited several unarticulated questions. For instance, I wondered how individuals whose sense of personhood is shaped by the presence and now the shadow of lynching trees develop the physical, mental, and spiritual fortitude to withstand the atrocities of a society that is in denial about its past. I also wanted to understand how persons who are subjected constantly to actual or potential acts of violence acquire a sense of self by which they are empowered to give voice to memories that present an alternative depiction of life in the United States. A significant concern is why survival of the fittest, especially as it pertains to people of the African diaspora in a republic that is in actuality an oligarchy parading as a democracy, is so often associated with struggle. I wanted to better understand the source of individual and collective strength that enables a people to avoid being consumed when terror is always present. These were some of my concerns as my tour guides and I returned to New Zion CME to listen and *reason together* about life in the shadow of the lynching tree. When asked to describe this community symbol, replete with philosophical-biblical-dogma life-negating experiences, Reverend Kidd, born September 14, 1936, in Benton, Louisiana, said:

> I am emotional right now because I had to walk past that hangman's tree that we pointed out that was out in the lake in the evenings, many times when it was dark and I was only a youngster going to get coal oil for the lights. . . . Walking past that hangman's tree was very, very frightening and intimidating. It gave me, most of

the time, a feeling of excruciating fear. Not only that—it seemed to go as deep as I can imagine. I would not be able to put in words. The innermost part of myself was frightened beyond the ability almost to move. The hurt didn't just last then—it was dehumanized. It made you think, what would happen and what could happen when you were in the company of whites. It was always there. It would give you this intestinal ache on the inside of your body. That's how I felt—scared stiff.[51]

Reverend Kidd's sister, Margie Kidd Campbell, born September 6, 1938, in Benton, Louisiana, shared that "every time we passed that tree, it wasn't—you just had to look up because you had a feeling what went on there. That was awful—an awful feeling."[52]

Then, at seventy-three and seventy-one years old, respectively, Kidd's and Campbell's memories of life in the shadow of the lynching tree raise questions about character formation in a camouflaged society. Their narrative accentuates why it is imperative to be aware of who determines whose testimonies will become a part of this country's heritage. In other words, it is imperative that black people not defer to someone else to determine whose worldview will influence subsequent generations' sense of self. Of utmost importance is how this selective subjective process can influence a person's ability to ascertain the effect that other voices, not included in what many accept unquestionably as the classical ethical canon that privileges varied configurations of whiteness, have on moral formation.

Imagine walking past killing sites on a daily basis. Imagine living in communities where killing or the possibility of killing at the hands of known persons is a daily reality. Each errand that required Clarence Kidd to walk past a lynching tree required him to rely on an inner strength that defied logic as he weighed the possibility of death, endemic to lynching culture, as antithetical to his own emerging sense of personhood. As black people walk past killing sites and view them on social media and other technological platforms, may the memory of victims and survivors of lynching and neo-lynching compel us to (a) act in a manner that always questions the subjective nature of fairness and justice, (b) be consistently compassionate, and (c) embody authenticity.

Memories of lynching and a culture of lynching are not the stories of fairy tales. One too many persons in the United States are reluctant to acknowledge this dark side of our national history. To cultivate a climate of *blind obedience* in the twenty-first century is to create police forces that are symbolic lynching trees. As a prerequisite to healing, lynching must be named as a national sin. A case study approach can be employed to address the fear lynching instilled in some and a sense of racialized entitlement lynching fostered in others. For instance, I can contrast Reverend Kidd's memories of a lynching tree in his community against police presence in what some describe as high crime rate areas. When translated, this inevitably is synonymous with poor urban black communities as a way to distract attention from affluent neighborhoods, for instance, that left many destitute in the wake of a yet unfolding banking fiasco.

From Kidd I learn that being *scared stiff* can motivate black people to exercise agency and join with others to dismantle systems of white supremacy whose continued prominence in this country is contingent on instilling fear-induced immobilization. Lynching in the nineteenth and twentieth centuries left no one unaffected. We need only glace at postcards of some of these public spectacles[53] to realize that children gathered at the base of hanging trees carry with them, as does Kidd, deeply embedded memories. My conversation with Walter Kidd and others in a Shreveport, Louisiana suburb is a poignant reminder that chambers of horror and death, though hidden in plain sight, are etched forever in the recesses of the mind. Several elders who entrusted a portion of their life stories to me are very much aware of the economics of a lynch culture sustained by an interlocking cycle of race and class. Thus, I was not surprised that Kidd and others in his generation thought they would not live to see the election of a person who is phenotypically black.

I watched with astonishment and disbelief as individuals figuratively removed their white-supremacist masks during the 2008 presidential campaign. This move, which continues to unfold during the 2016 presidential campaign, advances a legacy of lynch culture that has, for centuries, been skillfully cultivated by architects who perpetuate xenophobia as a means to manipulate, exploit, and control persons who lack the intellectual capacity needed to engage in an informed class analysis. While more attention can and should be given to dimensions of patriarchy, Mrs. Emma Kidd proclaimed that one is able to speak truth, even when under siege, when "God is on our side."[54] Or as Reverend Kidd put it,

> I knew God was there. That's the only way that I could live through this stuff is that God was always there with me causing me to even receive sometimes what could be thought of as blessing because many times I saw the whites treating others a different way and when they would come to me, they'd talk to me like I was a human being.

According to Reverend Kidd, this observed behavior "was from beyond."[55] It is quite possible that he is correct. However, I want to suggest that people of faith are called to be on God's side.

In a similar vein, a cross-theology and cross-ethic is grounded in an existential reality of everyday ordinary people. It is a reality premised upon the United States' global capitalistic system of exploitation. Certainly, in a country where blood courses through the memories of a people descended from persons legally designated as chattel, as human cargo, many can benefit from insights of persons who speak candidly about lynching. While some "Remembering Lynching" participants are "hopeful that it will be even better in the future,"[56] it is imperative not to equate prayer with behavior that is void of human action. While some oral history contributors "hope that God will deliver us one day,"[57] it is incumbent upon everyone to cultivate multigenerational alliances to confront evil. As black people "look for a better day" with anticipation that "it will come,"[58] a rereading of these oral histories suggests it is imperative to remember as well as to listen and hear this story of life in the United States to which some persons have no desire to return.

4

Unrelenting Tenacity

In the Shadow of the Lynching Tree

T he words of Sweet Honey in the Rock's "Ella's Song" are a reminder that "we who believe in freedom cannot rest; we who believe in freedom cannot rest until it comes. Until the killing of black men, black mothers' sons is as important as the killing of white men, white mothers' sons; we who believe in freedom cannot rest; we who believe in freedom cannot rest until it comes."[1] As I mentioned in the first chapter, I recorded oral histories with individuals who live in Alexandria, Hampton, Norfolk, Occoquan, Richmond, and Woodbridge (Virginia); Sumter (South Carolina); Hillside, Linden, and Roselle (New Jersey); Omaha (Nebraska); Oklahoma City (Oklahoma); Dallas (Texas); Bossier City, Gilbert, Lake Charles, Minden, Monroe, Shreveport, and Winnsboro (Louisiana); Hayward and Oakland (California); Philadelphia (Pennsylvania); and Birmingham (Alabama). Each contributor, shaped by a story that emerges from and is informed by

both a specific and a shared understanding of life in the United
States of America, participates in the cultivation and dissem-
ination of knowledge as a creative process that requires me
to think long and hard about what functions as authoritative
sources for moral discernment.[2] While they have breath in
their body, these human repositories of cultural-historical
data exhibit a remarkable ability to go deep into their interior in order to excavate historical truths that can function as
socioreligious markers. From their stories, I retrieve useable
data I employ to interpret present dilemmas so that I can,
individually and collectively, participate in the unfolding of a
more hope-filled future for all of creation. As I listen to each
account and read the associated transcript, I do so mindful that each lynching narrative is a primary text. As such,
priority must be given to both the interviewee's contextual
location(s) and the sociocultural factors that might influence
how a story is transmitted and the level of detail offered. In
addition, there is a preponderance of sociological[3] evidence,
for instance, that confirms that actions designed to manufacture a fear of death are tantamount to perpetuating a culture
of lynching. While we may replace the rope and fagot of the
late nineteenth and early to mid-twentieth centuries with
other killing instruments, the message that not all human life
is valued, that black life does not matter, persists. Although
persons may not hang from an oak tree on the courthouse
lawn or other public spaces for hours, the body of an unarmed
teenager lying in the streets for hours conveys to many that
lynching is etched into the DNA of this nation.[4] When concerned citizens inquire about actions that lead to a fatal outcome, a typical answer is to call for a state of emergency. From
increased police presence to activation of National Guard
units to control responses to the shooting of unarmed black

persons in the United States, I have yet to hear a journalist describe community members' immediate reactions to these atrocious acts as a public outcry against tyranny. Ironically, in the aftermath of what journalists and others dubbed "The Arab Spring,"[5] persons across the globe continue to talk about neo-lynching practices in the United States. This was most evident when Palestinians offered practical advice on various social media platforms to human rights activists on ways to minimize the effects of tear gas during a government-ordered occupation in Ferguson, Missouri. For instance, activists in the Middle East used Twitter and other social media platforms to provide specific directions—from tips on how to remain calm when tear gas is released in a crowd to how much distance to maintain between protestors and police.[6] In this age of neo-lynching, an individual's credentials and accomplishments, *accepted forms of compliance*, and *prescribed modes of orderly engagement* are no guarantees that black lives matter. Perhaps, this is why lynching should be of importance to the church in the twenty-first century.

Individuals who employ nonviolent direct confrontation that mirrors strategies used during the 1960s civil rights movement bear witness to the church's prophetic mandate. When they speak truth to people in positions of power, today's activists unveil the extent of hypocrisy embedded in US policies at local, state, and national levels that places black lives in a constant state of danger. Today's activists talk in plain language so that anyone who hears may understand what is at stake and make a decision whether to feign ignorance or speak truth. As black citizens and others confront systems of injustice with the intent to dismantle disparate systems that govern life in the United States, their complaint resonates with that of the prophet Habakkuk. As persons give voice 150 years after congress ratified the Thirteenth Amendment to abolish slavery, many ask, "How long shall I cry for help, and you will not listen? Or cry to you 'Violence!' and you will not save?"[7] They utter these pleas for intervention as they embody simultaneously manifestations of active faith. Aware of consequences associated with speaking truth to persons in positions of power, prophetic responses in the form of protests, die-ins, critiques, documentaries, sermons, speeches, and publications highlight the magnitude of a system whose practices of injustice sanction government-sponsored forms of domestic terrorism.

When active-duty and retired police officers who serve(d) with integrity choose not to denounce publicly these neo-lynching practices, their silence can be justifiably misinterpreted. Since silence is not necessarily an absence of courage, a reluctance to speak out might be an act of self-preservation or the evidence of fear for some. Yet this raises deeper concerns about the pervasiveness of violence as a basic characteristic of dehumanizing systems. After all, it is virtually impossible for any black person to determine how an individual who is charged to protect and serve will respond when encountered. Thus, to talk about race honestly in the United States is to talk about the lie upon which this nation is founded. I realize, though, that persons who most benefit from a social construction that advances whiteness as *the* normative standard may not want to engage in this dialogue. After all, to give voice to generations of unquestioned privilege will ultimately require the tough work of repentance as a prerequisite to forgiveness and reconciliation. To engage in such a conversation is to submit a classical ethical canon to examination. This cognitive dissonance recognizes a need to consider the limitations of a closed canon. African Americans who remember lynching and a culture of lynching can draw attention to the significance of ascertaining the effect that other voices may have on moral formation. From the memories of persons formed in the shadow of lynching trees, I glean insights about character and fortitude that enable persons to imagine hope-filled possibilities for themselves and others.

Remembering Lynching: "Can't forget the past"

A military veteran and deacon in the Church of God in Christ, Junius Nottingham Sr. resides in the Southwest Philadelphia row house in which he and his late wife, Dorcas Dorothy Nottingham, raised their four children. He purchased his home in the late 1950s on the G.I. Bill and worked several jobs upon leaving the army. The "second black to be hired in the plumbing department," Nottingham retired from the Philadelphia Board of Education on January 2, 1998, after almost thirty years of service. Some might say that his children defy the odds with undergraduate degrees from Temple, Drexel, and West Chester Universities. Because he and his wife "knew the importance of education," their "kids knew that it was not going to be twelve years of schooling, and then that was it. We explained either college, trade school, business school, military."

Living in a sector of the city that has a 36.4 percent poverty rate with only 7.2 percent of its residents college graduates,[8] Nottingham insists that lynching must be a concern for the church in the twenty-first century "because once you lose sight on history you cannot go to the future. Because if you lose sight on the past, you're going to go into the future, and if you're not careful, you're going to be doing some of the same things that happened in the past." Born November 27, 1933, in Cape Charles, Virginia, on the "eastern shore . . . right before you cross the Chesapeake Bay to go into Norfolk," Nottingham speaks frankly about a need to recall the insidious nature of lynching culture.

All too often, as in Nottingham's case, memories of lynching are transmitted across generations. Speaking about his earliest recollection of this cultural practice, he explains:

> [My] grandfather said as a boy he saw many a man lynched. He said if some of the men would talk back or either if they act like they didn't want to do what "the white man said do," they were lynched. And, my grandfather said they couldn't do anything about it, because they had no control. So, it was more or less they saw, but they could not speak.[9]

Although Nottingham's grandfather may not have spoken out publicly, this recounting serves as evidence that a type of talking took place that may merit further analysis to determine how or whether this form of transmission is reflective of practices associated with religious practices of formerly enslaved persons, most notably embodied expressions associated with hush harbors.[10] Nottingham stated that as a life-preserving measure his grandfather also

> shared with [Nottingham] that often times that they would see men go down the road as if they were going home. They would never see them anymore. But then word would get back, so-and-so had been lynched. And, he said his mother and father—certain times, they would not allow him to go into the woods, because they knew that it was men that had been lynched—in the woods.

This cultural awareness led Nottingham as an adult stationed in Germany in 1955 to talk candidly about his own angry response to Emmett Till's lynching. According to Nottingham, upon receipt of this news he and other black soldiers "were angry, not to the point where [they] wanted to go out and do something destructive. But [they] also knew that this was the policy of the South." For Nottingham and others who lived during this reign of terror, they learned about this prescriptive way of life through "stories from some of the older men in [his] church, where, like if you looked at a white woman, even to speak, if you're not careful, you would be lynched." As he continued to reflect on his initial reaction to Emmett Till's death, Nottingham said, "[I and my fellow soldiers] didn't take it with a grain of salt, but we took it with anger, but we also knew—this was reality. And, how we were going to combat it, we had no idea." The questions with which Nottingham wrestled in 1955 are sadly still relevant in 2016. As the United States continues to advance toward a police-occupied nation, it is imperative that I, like Nottingham, acknowledge and voice concerns about this moral problem. As he stated, "So, it's just like, you see injustice done, but you are—you're upset about it, but now—who has the answer? What can we do to prevent this from happening again?"

Nottingham's recollection of lynching suggests, in a manner similar to Rosalie Joseph's account of her brother's escape, that running was a viable option. This was the case for an individual who, in his nineties, told his story of migration as a life-preserving strategy to Nottingham, who says:

> Now, talking about the lynching, there was a deacon in
> my church, Deacon Harrison Byrd. And, as a boy—and
> he said his mother would take in laundry for the white

woman down the road. And when she would finish, he would have to take their laundry down in a wagon. He would take it down, and he said—but every time he would take it down, the woman would make him get in the bed with her. And, he said—he told her, "I can't do this." And she told him, "If you don't, I'm going to tell them you raped me." So he said, he had to do it. He said—but one day he went into town, and he heard the white men talking, how they were going to hang him up, because somehow or another, they must have gotten wind of what was going on. And he said he was so afraid, he came home, he told his mother, he said, "I'm leaving." He said he left [North Carolina] that day, came to Philadelphia. He never went back home.

With a profound understanding of lynching and societal norms, Nottingham "feels so put out because these things happened." He speaks not only about events that happened to others but also about a very deep and personal account that occurred when he and his wife traveled to Virginia in 1956 to attend his uncle's funeral. On their way back to Philadelphia, they stopped at a store, and Nottingham recalls:

And that's when the white man in the store grabbed my wife by her behind, and was squeezing her behind. And she said she was so afraid, she just didn't say anything—just stood right there. So, she told me when we got half way home. And then I was angry with her— but then after I realized that she said, "I thought about what had happened to Emmett Till." She said, "And I didn't want that to happen to you." So after I calmed down, I said, "It makes sense." Because if I had beat that man—listen, before we got to Philadelphia, they would have had the state police, and everybody, and

took me right back there—probably would've beat me
up, and maybe—hung me up, because this was in '56.

His wife's response to this act of horizontal violence and Nottingham's subsequent concurrence with her immediate reaction to this hostile and aggressive behavior reflect myriad
ways in which black women have been exempt from notions
of female respectability. In order to survive further repercussions associated with this sexual assault, Dorothy Nottingham had to consider in a matter of seconds how to preserve
both her own and her husband's life. This strategy to engage
in a process of mind shifting served as a coping mechanism
by which persons subjected to oppressive behaviors did not
assume responsibility for perpetrators' actions. For Nottingham, this realization caused him to recognize the enormity of
his wife's decision.

Troubled by "the fact that our young black children today
have no idea of what their grandparents, great-grandparents
had to go through," Nottingham refers to his memories
of lynching as

> a learning experience, but on the other hand, you don't
> want to question God, but in a sense, you have to. And
> I don't think he's going to hold it against us, because
> we do question him. Job questioned him, but he didn't
> give Job an answer. So, we can question him. It doesn't
> mean he'll answer, but . . . he's still in control. And
> although, we have been beat, killed, whipped . . . he's
> going to deliver us out of this. Don't ask me how, I have
> no idea. But in his word, he says he's the God of all
> flesh. And then he asks the question, "Is anything too
> hard for me?" And, oftentimes, we have to stop and lis-
> ten. Is anything too hard for him?

In the midst of pervasive evil, Nottingham places his trust in a God who is a liberator. At the same time, Nottingham espouses an active faith that is lived out, in part, through a commitment "to talk about things that has happened." As Nottingham explains, "It's so much that we have experienced, especially those of us that are seventy and older—you know, because we were children, but still we remember these things, like that."[11]

Like Nottingham, most oral history participants talk candidly about why lynching should be discussed. Their stance is based on a premise which expresses their concern that

- young people can know where we came from[12] . . .
- there is a need to know what happened in the yesteryears[13] . . .
- they don't think we should hold anything back[14] . . .
- if you forget the past there is nothing you can do[15] . . .
- people never forget that there were certain human rights that we were denied, and they didn't come easy[16] . . .
- everyone needs to be told the story[17] . . .
- young people need to know about this because they don't have any idea.[18]

From his act of remembering and sharing, Junius Nottingham Sr. reminds me that as persons in the twenty-first century work to dismantle systems that sustain neo-lynching practices, they will do well to be mindful to "build on your strength. And all of us have strengths. It may not be the same. Build on what you can do"[19] always with a present informed by the past as a guide toward what is yet to come.

Contextualized Faith: "Suffering is reality"

When asked to define faith, most African American elders who self-identify as Christian quote Hebrews 11:1: "Now faith is the substance of things hoped for, the evidence of things not seen."[20] This verse reminds oral history participants that human-orchestrated atrocities should not serve as a deterrent to detract persons from participating in God's unfolding plan for humanity. African American elders who came of age during the United States' epoch of lynching in the early to mid-twentieth century find assurance in this biblical verse. There is a confident hope contained in these sacred words that to ignore the severity of lynching culture designed to diminish black people's sense of themselves as persons created fully in God's image is a sin. In the case of Reverend Zan Wesley Holmes Jr., elected to complete the term of "the first African American from Dallas to be elected to the legislature since reconstruction,"[21] addressing "issues in the community"[22] was not optional.

The son of a United Methodist pastor, Holmes was born in San Angelo, Texas, on February 1, 1935. His family relocated to Waco when he was nine months old, approximately nineteen years after Jesse Washington was lynched there.[23] When asked initially to discuss his earliest memory of lynching, Holmes replied:

> Well, that's why I wonder why you have me here. I—you know, my parents sheltered me—us. I mean, we were there. My father was a pastor in the city, but we stayed on our side of town and I cannot remember any real major bad experiences I had as a child in terms of racial discrimination or violence or anything because—you know, after I grew up, I looked back and I saw how my parents protected me from that. They just shielded us from that. We had very limited contacts with whites.[24]

A conscious decision to withhold details of racial violence was a strategy employed by several parents of individuals whose oral memoirs comprise the "Remembering Lynching" collection. Adults held this deliberate act designed to shelter and protect in tension with lessons on how children should behave in order not to attract unwanted attention.

Holmes did not learn about this lynching in Waco until he attended Huston–Tillotson University in Austin, Texas. He said, "[Knowledge of this horrific incident caused me to] wonder why I didn't hear anything about that. Nobody talked about that. And my parents—I was thirteen years old when I left [Waco], but I didn't hear anything about it. You know, I found out about that." Holmes did not indicate, nor did I ask, if his parents read black-owned newspapers that chronicled lynchings. Holmes discovered subsequently that the father of his friend, "Rene Martinez who works with the Dallas Independent School District . . . spent time in Waco and witnessed that [Jesse Washington's lynching]." According to Holmes, Martinez told him, "My father was there. He saw that. He witnessed that." Holmes explains:

> [Martinez shared] how angry his father was—he tried to help me understand how his father was really engaged in the struggle of social justice. But that was one of the things that his father told him about, how disturbed he was about that. Now, that was the first time I had talked to someone who knew someone who witnessed that and again, I was just, you know, just shocked by all of that.

In addition, Holmes recalls:

> [When] Waco elected a black woman mayor . . . they had a picture of this hanging there in the city hall. It was still hanging there and how she protested that. I

think they finally removed it or something. But you know, the scandalous tidbits of information and stuff like that—so I've just followed that. But again, I guess it still bothered me that that was not a part—that whole story was not a part of the—you know, nobody talked about that.

With graduate theological degrees from Perkins School of Theology at Southern Methodist University in Dallas, Texas, and more than two decades experience as a pastor and professor, Holmes grasps the significance of lynching as a metaphor to control human behavior. As his narrative makes clear, his parents and other African American adults did not

> talk about that because it accomplished what lynching was designed to accomplish. To strike fear in the hearts and souls and minds of black folk, to intimidate black people. . . . And black folk just didn't talk about it. They just didn't, many of them. Maybe some did, but many black folk didn't talk about it. Because see, I'm told that they dragged that body all in the community. They did that, drug the body around. I don't know how true that is but they—that they did that again just to strike fear in hearts of the black community, you know, stay in their place. And I think, maybe also, like my father and my mother, they thought that that might have some negative impact upon us and they didn't want us to have that same fear and so . . . they didn't tell the story because they wanted to forget it and because they thought it might have some negative impact upon us.

The second oldest of his parents' six children, Holmes "never had an opportunity to talk with [his] parents about that."

Conversations with his siblings about Waco's 1916 lynching revealed that they "hadn't heard anything about it either."[25]

Pastor of St. Luke "Community" United Methodist Church in Dallas, Texas, from 1974 to 2002, Holmes was instrumental in helping the congregation to become intentional in its desire to "be advocates and prophetic voices in the community for all underserved and oppressed peoples."[26] It is therefore not surprising that, given Holmes' personal involvement in social justice-related issues, lynching has informed his understanding of justice. As he explains,

> To even just see pictures, and I've seen pictures of—it is—first, angry. The anger that I felt to just see that and then to try to imagine those persons who were hanged, what that must have felt like to them, to be mutilated, to be able to have their lives destroyed like that, and to be—to go through that. It's identification, in a way. . . . There was some identification with those people. And also, it's almost like that could have been anybody, any black person, any of us. It could have been me. I mean, . . . because it's such a random kind of thing. People were accused for nothing. That just couldn't—that fact—just to think about what it might have been to live in a time like that, when that could happen and the community could gather and it became a public event and people could celebrate it.

Holmes' analysis reflects the extent of lynching culture as a mechanism by which to obliterate black lives by any available means. Not only did these acts of domestic terror happen in the previous century, they continue to occur on a frequent basis in 2016. At a time when black lives were and continue to be devalued, Holmes discusses what lynching "does to the value of life." By explicitly stating black "lives meant nothing," Holmes draws correlations to modern-day experiences. By juxtaposing references to historical lynchings, Holmes speaks directly about current realities that affect the value of black lives. He acknowledges, "[Lynching is] a very painful thing to just think about and to think that the consequences of that [are] just as real today. I think it happened then and it can happen again because the same forces that were at work then are at work now." Furthermore, Holmes maintains:

> [A culture of lynching has caused me to] struggle with why and how do I explain that in terms of faith. And to some extent to see Jesus on the other hand, as one who was crucified unjustly, see him as one who identifies— can identify with that rate of the lynching. And to the injustice of that, of his death and to see that as the center of our faith, that death, that crucifixion, as the center of our faith and to see the resurrection as a way of life coming out of that—victory coming out of that or to put it this way, to just understand how one can be a good steward of one's suffering for the sake of a brand new future.

This stance raises questions about passive faith in which persons internalize trauma and become complicit in their oppression. While a focus on self as suffering servant moving toward a non-oppressive future may provide a measure of assurance to Holmes, he also addresses the tension with which he contends. He finds that "it continues to be a struggle, because how do we preach to people who are still going through that kind of stuff? And every day, how do we preach to them? How do we give them hope?" These are questions with which every person engaged in the difficult work of justice, in a country where mass shootings and police misconduct are remaining the norm, must struggle. Strengthened by his faith, Holmes does not give lynching the final word. He holds firm to the belief that "we can live in spite of that. And we serve a God who identifies with pressures and who gives us the power to overcome that." Given his hope-filled stance, Holmes insists:

> [Lynching] should be a major concern for the Church because it's at the heart of the Christian faith. . . . Why do the innocent suffer? It's an act of exploitation. . . . The life and death of Jesus really symbolizes that for me. . . . I follow the crucified savior because we can identify with the crucified savior and . . . that's why religion that does not make that identity . . . to me is just inauthentic. It cannot be real for people who continue to suffer today. And people who know that story, the lynching story—it cannot be real. Suffering is reality.[27]

Suffering as a reality for many African Americans continues to be shaped by a culture of lynching. To address techniques that devalue black lives, faith-formed responses must emerge from contextual experiences of everyday encounters with violence. These solutions demand we rethink whose voice matters and necessitate that we create space for a multiplicity of views to be heard. To confront this painful fact that black lives do not matter is a process of divestiture and realignment in which persons seek simultaneously to embody daily that which is just. This is no easy feat in a society where perceived respectability often outweighs treating persons with dignity. For such a time as this, people of faith can ill afford to describe acts of terrorism, particularly those sanctioned by government at all levels, in general terms. To do so further erodes the value of human life, even our very own lives.

Then and Now: "Time we face reality"

African American elders' descriptions of lynching culture substantiate why we cannot ignore inhumane practices. They are adamant that "times are critical now."[28] As such, a close read of their accounts suggests it is imperative to learn how to read silence carefully and critically. Prior to acts of civil disobedience in the aftermath of Michael Brown's death, an African American elder aptly noted that failure to comprehend and respond in positive ways to the enormity of growing distrust among black people is necessary "in order to possibly prevent a reoccurrence."[29] Life experience compels some African American elders to disavow adamantly "turning our backs on it rather than facing it head on."[30] It is difficult for many of them, as they observe the erosion of civil liberties for which some of them risked their lives and from which many benefitted, not to conclude that a culture of terror that was prevalent during their formative years is "still happening."[31] Thus, there is an urgency that ought to compel us to talk about our country's fraught history of violence. First and foremost is that it is "time that we face reality"[32] and ask ourselves whether we have an obligation to tell multiple generations about lynching or, as one participant asserted, "to keep this before them."[33]

Born on June 2, 1931, in Arcadia, Louisiana, "a place that was made famous by Bonnie and Clyde,"[34] Reverend Dr. L. P. Lewis declares, "[Lynching] was an experience that I'll never be able to get out of my mind." In response to my question about his earliest memory of lynching, Lewis replies:

> When I was around six years old our neighbor's sister's
> son was ultimately lynched. . . . The trauma that that
> involves surrounded this whole event. When we heard

that the police were looking for his nephew—and when stuff like that happened it become customary that the black community was like, on lockdown—that you stayed in your house, you locked the door, you closed the door, and they were—the grownups were very careful about how they talked about it.

Lewis' description of a community under siege in approximately 1937 is eerily similar to desired responses by residents in occupied neighborhoods in the United States in 2016. In a manner reminiscent of Junius Nottingham Sr., Lewis' recounting of events highlights a child's capacity to retain and process information. He offers the following details about this lynching that took place in the outskirts of Ruston, Louisiana, about eighteen miles east of Arcadia in Lincoln Parish:

And what happened is that our neighbor's nephew supposedly assaulted a white woman down sort of in the country. . . . Well, we knew where that was—there was a lot of farming and stuff. And so some white lady accused him—I'm trying to remember his name; I can't remember[35]—of assaulting—or trying to assault or rape her. The other story was he was walking—this came, evidently, from him. He was off walking in the woods, and he walked up on this couple—on the white man and white woman, and they were undressed and participating in something, and he saw it. And people were of the belief that something had to be done because he saw it. And the story goes that she—whatever she concocted up—that he approached her. And so it was all of that going on for two or three days. And finally, when they found him hiding in a barn amongst the hay and all of that they brought him out and in the heat of the—this mob found the nearest tree they could find

and hanged him, and burned him I'm told, and then
dragged his body through the town.

Similar to Wallace Hartsfield Sr., who recalled a lynching
that occurred in his Georgia community when he was eight
or nine, Lewis' earliest memory of lynching was a defining
moment in his moral formation. Not naïve about segregated
life, Lewis found himself at a young age learning to negotiate
and navigate in a society where his well-being was not a consideration. In many respects, Lewis and other African American children in his era learned how to survive life in a combat
zone. It was, he says,

> how we were prepared. I mean there was an era of
> fear—that you stayed in the house, don't you go out the
> house, lock the door, want to make sure nothing hap-
> pens to you. And it's like a horror story that humanity
> can inflict such a thing upon humanity. And that was
> just so sad that you had no recourse. You had no day
> in court. It's you go by what somebody said, and based
> upon what they say, the vigilante groups got together.
> And so that was always that fear, and I was very care-
> ful during the time I lived in segregated society that
> I always would, when I walk up and down the streets
> uptown and the white race would come by—man or
> woman, boy or girl, you get off the sidewalk. Let them
> walk. So I was always careful of those things that—in
> fact, I would never hardly look at them.

Lewis notes that his parents "talked quietly about" this
lynching. Like several participants mentioned, Lewis con-
curs, "There was a way when older people talked that they
dismissed the children. . . . But they normally wouldn't

discuss these things. They would just give us advice in terms of how we should conduct ourselves, so [we] could keep out of harm's way." Then, as now, survival of black people is contingent upon an ability to negotiate public spaces inhabited by persons who can, without notice, change the rules of engagement. Now, as then, black people can be randomly targeted for undisclosed or unjustifiable reasons and subjected to the whims of persons who can manipulate and destroy evidence. Then, as now, there is a level of fear from which no sector of black life is exempt. To live in a society in which eye contact can be interpreted as an act of defiance rather than an acknowledgment of another's humanity signals that now is the time to confront the reality of this moment in history. Irrespective of advice given "in terms of how to protect ourselves and avoid trouble,"[36] now, as then, we can never prepare fully for the onslaught of evil that seeks to destroy the very essence of black existence in this republic.

Perhaps this is why Lewis encourages us to remember two things that should be of importance to the church in the twenty-first century. First, he implores us never to forget "the courage, and faith, and the tenacity of our parents and our foreparents." Second, he says, "we should never forget that there were certain human rights that we were denied, and they didn't come easy. A lot of blood, sweat, and tears took place for these rights to come to fruition—i.e., just to vote." Lewis voices concern about a dearth of historical knowledge by a growing percentage of black people coupled with what he perceives as a decline in active community involvement. Lewis insists, "Things can happen if you don't stay active." Ultimately, he is concerned that "if we become complacent," individually and collectively it may become increasingly difficult to advance a movement orchestrated to effect

positive change in communities that are socially and economically challenged.

More important, given that we live in an era where a
criminal penal system continues to be marketed as a justice
system where persons are often perceived as guilty unless
they can prove otherwise, Lewis says:

> [I] came to the conclusion that the only thing that
> we really have to provide and to look after us was the
> grace and love of God, because everything else was
> not there for us. And the whole thing about justice was
> that justice, through the blessing of God, everything
> was divine for me, because justice did not exist—not
> for me. But faith in God, and the power of God—and I
> know that. God works in community with us.[37]

This concept of atonement, grounded in an understanding
of a divine human encounter, defies ways of knowing that
privilege physical sight. What Lewis asks me to consider is
whether I am willing to embrace an ability to see that which
may be invisible to the human eye but is yet accessible. It is a
way of seeing that may enable me to negotiate multiple realms
simultaneously. It is only when I am able to embark upon an
honest intimate relationship with the one in whose image I am
formed, mindful that my way of being is but one expression of
divine encounter, that I am empowered to face the reality that
life in the persistent shadow of lynching trees, though fraught
with pain, propels me to count the costs of my actions.

Exemplars of Moral Living:
"We can make a difference"

When I reflect on African American elders' rationale to support their stance that lynching should be of concern for the

church in the twenty-first century, I am struck by their ability to recall a time when the church was a "vehicle for educating our people."[38] Whether they are engaged congregants in historically black churches or ecclesial bodies characterized as mainline protestant organizations, "Remembering Lynching" participants recall a time when the church served as a primary "instrument in the community to step forward and lay its hands on whatever situation is taking place."[39] For them, the "Church ought to be the voice that raises its concern."[40] What this stance presumes is that rules that guide personal and communal life are informed by principles that do not view black life as tangential. Perhaps as a response to hate-filled rhetoric from one who aspires to be the forty-fifth president of the United States,[41] African American elders who lived during a time when reports of lynching dominated the news cycle might admonish "church leaders [to] provide some type of instrument that will encourage their congregations to organize, or whatever necessary, to prevent such events from occurring."[42] If the church is called to be a "mechanism where black people should get guidance,"[43] lynching, neo-lynching, and "any wrong should be discussed at church."[44] Such observations suggest that "the church is a community where people come together, and we've been taught from the Bible that you're supposed to love everybody."[45]

Unlike Clarence Kidd and his sister, Margie Kidd Campbell, who are life-long residents of the Shreveport metropolitan area, Myrtle E. Ballard's memory of lynching is not informed by a community symbol of terror. Ballard was born on April 20, 1930, in Shreveport, Louisiana, and her knowledge of lynching may be attributed to some degree to her family's relocation to Oakland, California, when she was approximately six years old. Since she returned to Shreveport, "the last place where the Confederacy surrendered,"[46] at least annually to visit relatives who resided in the Hollywood neighborhood, her knowledge of lynching does point to a manner in which migrant communities remained informed about events related to their homes of origin. As Ballard notes,

> When I was about—I think I was thirteen—I lived in Oakland, but we used to read the papers from Shreveport. And in Oakland when I was a child, there was a whole group of people from Shreveport. . . . And I guess we read the newspaper and everything, and I think there was a soldier that was stationed in Bossier City, and something happened, and I can't even remember what happened. They electrocuted him in Shreveport, and that was in the paper. And that was just shocking to me. But that was the only thing that I remember.

Ballard does not recall any conversations about this incident among community members. According to her,

> There was just—they had read it, and it was awful, and that was it. They just left it. So, I never knew any more about it, but he was stationed in Bossier City. I can remember that. And he was young. They had his picture in the paper and everything. And something happened, and I can't even remember what happened that they actually did it right in the city of Shreveport in the courthouse.[47]

Through her fifty-plus years of civic engagement, Ballard, who has been a Methodist for the majority of her life, has been unwavering in her stance that the church is called to epitomize personal and social holiness in its teaching and its actions. Thus, when it comes to lynching, she implores the church to embrace its prophetic nature. Unequivocally, Ballard states:

> I think that the church would be the place that could really be against this openly, and maybe not a lot of things would happen to the people in the church for that. And then the Church is united. . . . It's a whole group of people. It's in an organization, like the National Baptist Convention. That's a lot of folks, and a lot of people paying taxes and stuff. And maybe that— and I think that the church as a group could stop a lot of things, and maybe that's the reason we should be worried about it, because—or even concerned about it, because we know that when we got together as a church, we could stop so many things.

Ballard's observations about the nature and function of the church suggest that people of faith, "can make a difference."[48]

While there are "many things churches can do to help the situation,"[49] Ballard's ecclesiological perspective is informed by a commitment to social justice. Accepting this notion as a given allows the church to be an exemplar for moral life. At the same time, Simon Morgan realizes, "No one can tell what's in the heart of a person in the first place. The church, I guess, has as part of its responsibility to change a person's persona. I guess to make that person a better person, better people; beyond that I'm not sure."[50] In its employment of Scripture as a source for moral discernment, the church embodies an understanding of itself as the body of Christ. When Christians pray *Lord your will be done on earth*, subsequent actions convey the church's intentions toward those who are impoverished, enslaved, incarcerated, misinformed, and/or oppressed. For this reason, it is with unrelenting tenacity that the church assumes its responsibility to work as an agent of change. As such, the church is aware that as an exemplar of moral living its responses to injustices are indicative of the church's relationship with the divine. With an openness to engage in a process of self-examination, African American elders' memories of lynching culture can serve as a guide for the church. Far from passive submission, when the church embraces a call to remove the veil of ignorance around matters of intersecting realities of race, gender, identity, and other artificial configurations, it takes an active stance against sin that is couched in white-supremacy ideology. In a context where all lives are not valued equally, when the church elects to confront systemic evil it does so with a persistent resolve to be a bearer of a truth that demands that it identify and name correctly "the cosmic powers of this present darkness."[51] In an age when religion is proffered by some as a criteria by which to engage in exclusionary practices, African American elders who remember lynching call on the church to address an erosion of civil and human liberties in the United States in such a way that this response will serve as a beacon of light that will propel others to align themselves with those whose very lives are at risk. Ultimately, to deny the humanity of one is to negate the image of God that is in each person. May the church, as an exemplar of moral living, not let this be so!

5

Lessons, Concerns, Hopes

Embodying an Ethic of Resilient Resistance

hrough a process of immersion into memories that I correlate with baptism, I continue to benefit from the experiences of persons whose oral histories are central to my ethical-theological analysis of lynching and a culture of lynching in the United States of America. Surprisingly, a close read of Martin Collins' narrative points to this ordinance in a manner that invites a critical examination of literal, liturgical, ethical, and metaphorical connotations. Collins is the only participant who did not self-identify as Christian. He also did not provide any indicators that he in any way was affiliated with a form of organized religion. Collins' memory of lynching culture pushes me to think about how a sacrament of the church should inform the rules that govern communal life. He does, after all, remind me that "no black people much in the South knew anything about justice—there was no justice—not for a black person."[1]

My baptism into "Remember Lynching" participants' memories of a time when "everybody was programmed to understand that—they wasn't going to do nothing to them"[2] is best characterized as a process of healing. Though symbolic, my engagement in this process of immersion signals my willingness to examine ways in which a preservation of African American elders' memories of lynching and a culture of lynching illustrates in concrete terms the importance of African American religious life as a fundamental aspect of US culture. Collins and other participants are clear about their experience of life in the shadow of the lynching tree. As Collins recounts:

> It was just the way of life for everybody—myself and everybody else. I was too young really to know it or think about it. It was just a way of life. You didn't have no rights or no freedom. Back then, most southern towns—up here too—if a black person was accused of something, you're supposed to be innocent until proven guilty. If some white person said or thought that you did something illegal, you were guilty of it right then without a trial. Say the police or somebody would tell that so-and-so did something or whatever, they would arrest you and wouldn't walk up to a black person and say, "You're under arrest," and take them to jail. They'd walk up to them with a club or something—billyclub or blackjack—and beat them to death and then throw them in the car and then get them out when they get to jail and beat them again and throw them in the jail cell. That was just the way of life.[3]

Whether participants had a direct memory of lynching or not, anyone who grew up in the United States in the early to mid-twentieth century grew up in a culture that was marked by an ever-present threat of mob rule, whether there were tangible signs of a lynching or not.[4] At the same time, there is no doubt that Collins and other participants are adamant that this is not the way life has to be or should be.

Far from acquiescing to life as imagined by architects of lynching and now proponents of a neo-lynching culture, oral history participants insist:

> Ignorance is not benevolent. It's not helpful. It doesn't advantage you. And it's like being anesthetized; you may not feel the pain but the injury is still there. So you are not being helped because you don't feel it. You can be beaten into unconsciousness and you may not feel it but the condition is there. So the rage within you, when you see things being done wrong, and you can't do anything about it. And you are expected to accept it. It's hard to accept something you know is wrong.[5]

For me, then, the existential reality of black life in the United States of America becomes a necessary starting point from which to (a) share lessons gleaned from participants' experiences, (b) articulate some of their concerns about how to navigate life in a neo-lynching culture, and (c) offer hope to young persons who are in a process of becoming their authentic selves.[6] From lessons, concerns, and hopes influenced by immersion in their memories, participants exemplify ways in which they embody an ethic of resilient resistance.

Participants confronted a world in which they were not expected to survive and certainly not to thrive. They learned, as Odell Carr remarked, how to "make the best out of what [they] [had] and what [they were] and then do the best that [they could] to help others."[7] Rather than a blind acquiescence to cultural dictates, participants' recollections of lynching and a culture of lynching highlight their willingness to speak truthfully about life. Their recounting of a pain-filled era, replete with contemporary residual manifestations, is evidence of a commitment to engage in an honest process that lends itself to a comparative analysis of personal values against values admired in other persons.

I contend this introspective work is often contingent on a personal decision to position myself to receive and value narratives that are not recognized typically as sources for Christian moral discernment. As I continue to sit with this body of historical data, I am awed by the capacity of the body, mind, and soul to recall detailed information that can expand and broaden knowledge about life in these United States of America. From these narratives, I gain insight about an ethic of resilient resistance that is rooted in a reality that transcends human logic. Resilient resistance refers to an ability to name and respond to evil in a manner that challenges practices that are neither just nor fair. It is an ethic for many oral history participants that is informed by faith. Reflecting on his own faith formation, Reverend L. P. Lewis says,

> My faith is still strong today because if we had not had the faith, God knows we wouldn't have a black president today. We had that faith. And even when we look at our parents, who could not read or write, but were able to fashion out a living of the throwaways and a lot of the stuff from the master's table, the part of the hog that they didn't want—we made a delicacy out of chitlins. Other stuff that they threw away that we could take it and make soup. And so this was but by the grace of God—because they didn't read text books—couldn't. But how did they know? How did they learn? And it was

through the guidance of the Holy Spirit; that's the only way. And so my faith was, no question, about the grace of God, and my faith in God because the other thing was not for me, and it was not appropriated to me, but God's love and faith in God's grace was always there.[8]

What I am suggesting is that an ethic of resilient resistance bears witness to a people's ability to read printed and cultural texts with remarkable depth in ways that give new meaning to masking and navigating when domestic terror tactics are disguised to placate and distract. What I am suggesting is that resilient resistance is a capacity to both respond in a manner that conveys a determination to fashion a life of grace filled possibilities and confront simultaneously evil personified in policies and practices. This ethic is a testimony of God's power to inspire black people and other subjugated persons to take what is meant for evil and transform it into a virtue such that other persons become skilled sociocultural interpreters.

In the shadow of twenty-first-century lynching trees, individuals who acknowledge the full humanity of all people are invited to seek creative and life-affirming ways to give voice to atrocities that continue to devalue black life. For such a time as this, the urgent question is not necessarily where is God in the midst of this entrenched pervasive evil. Rather, a serious concern is how to experience God, whose self-revelation in Jesus the Christ conveys that life and not death is the final word. This posture also necessitates that even if it is impossible to come to terms with death by hanging—whether an ancient-world crucifixion or a modern-day lynching—clarity about events that necessitate a reexamination of actions that thwart or advance notions of humanity is essential.

We are at a juncture in the United States where black people and persons aligned with us do not have the luxury to ignore cultural realities. African American elders who remember lynching implore us to "do [our] best each and every day, keep moving don't stop."[9] From lessons, concerns, and hopes shaped in the shadow of lynching trees, these elders reflect on what it means to be fully human. As I reviewed words of wisdom that participants wanted to share with future generations, four primary themes emerged. Each wisdom saying is a poignant reminder that black lives matter. Baptized in their memories, these elders' words of wisdom have the power to bridge generational differences and forge alliances.

Wisdom Saying #1: "Aim high"

One hundred and fifty years since Congress ratified the Thirteenth Amendment to abolish chattel slavery in the United States, African American elders who are not so distanced from lynching culture urge young black persons to "aim high."[10] While they would like this hope to be accepted as a given, oral history participants speak from a place of knowing that should not be dismissed without further investigation. Convinced that individuals "can be anything you want to be,"[11] some African American elders also insist that black people are still held to a higher standard than white people. For instance, retired army officer and educational administrator George Hampton says, "I remember when I was a kid, one of the things that the old folks used to say back in those days was, in order to be as good as they are—as good as them—you have to be better than them."[12]

Hampton, born June 7, 1928, in Englewood, New Jersey, relocated to Greensboro, North Carolina, in 1945. One of eight children, Hampton says,

[I] was a very serious juvenile delinquent when I was in Jersey. My mother passed away when I was fifteen,[13] and when my brother from Greensboro—he was a physician in Greensboro—when he came up for the funeral, he and my father talked about the situation with me, and so he and his wife decided that if my dad didn't mind, he'd take me back to Greensboro with him. That was the best thing that ever happened to me really because I had a chance to meet a totally new environment and get involved with—academically and came out very well out of high school and went on to college, which I probably—when I tell people today, if I hadn't gone to Greensboro, I'd probably be serving seven years to life in Rahway State Prison in New Jersey.

Hampton speaks frankly about socioeconomic realities that remain a pressing concern for many black people. Although he describes the decision to live with his brother as a defining moment in his life, Hampton also says, "[This transition and change in lifestyle] was a little difficult from time to time because there were quite a few confrontations with my brother with regard to what I wanted to do and how I wanted to do it." With explicit expectations and a system of accountability, with his "sister-in-law as the peacemaker,"[14] Hampton developed an appreciation for setting goals.

When they are establishing goals, Hampton does not want young black persons to succumb to the myth that the United States of America can be characterized as a post-racial society.[15] Instead, Hampton wants young black people to understand that post-racial rhetoric "is a mask." As he explains, "That's part of the same old, old song. You know, it's wait your turn, or things are coming, or things will get better soon."[16] Despite a pattern of socially constructed claims of racial inferiority, African American elders' act of truth telling is designed to convey to future generations why it is important to "always set a goal in your life."[17]

Irrespective of the level of formal education attained or chosen occupation, African American elders who remember lynching associate the notion to *aim high* with a capacity to "have a vision."[18] They want future generations to develop a level of self-confidence so they "let no one or anything stop [them] from achieving [their] goals."[19] Far from advocating a form of narcissistic individualism, African American elders advance a "you can"[20] attitude to inspire future generations to "do the best that [they] can and move forward."[21] After all, as Marguerite Harris maintains, "if you don't aim high—you may not get up to the very top, but if you hadn't aimed at all, you wouldn't get anywhere."[22]

When a Supreme Court justice refuses to acknowledge a distinction between affirmative action and substandard public school systems[23] that disproportionately disadvantage children who reside in economically depressed neighborhoods, these elders, as retired public school educator Dorothy Clark reflects, want future generations of black youth and young adults to imagine the impossible and to realize they can do and "be anything [they] want to be."[24] Irrespective of circumstances, these elders convey a message of hope to future generations. Rather than conform to caricatures of black life that demean and dehumanize, these elders are adamant in their insistence that younger generations "just keep going."[25] Ultimately, these elders do not want younger generations to "give up."[26] Instead, these elders want future generations to "do whatever [they] can. Do the best [they] can do each and every day and don't give up because of the small things that may be happening to [them]."[27]

At the end of the day, these elders want future generations to realize that to *aim high* is to embrace a mandate to
"live up to the best [they] can, and do the best [they] can"[28]
at all times. This can be difficult. After all, these elders are
very much aware that white-supremacist ideology remains a
threat irrespective of socioeconomic status. In addition, these
elders voice concern that ecclesial leaders and people of faith
have a responsibility to nurture within young black persons a
desire to live into a state of shalom that is shaped by an ideal
of justice that may require some to explore practical ways in
which to honor a theology of jubilee informed by, but not limited to, varied forms of reparations. Thus, from persons who
came of age in the shadow of lynching trees, future generations are compelled to remember that to *aim high* conveys a
determination to live each day with a conviction not to allow
anyone to deter them from accomplishing their individual
and collective goals. To the young generations of grassroots
activists who place their lives on the line, literally and metaphorically, these African American elders want to encourage
you to "stay with it, whatever you're doing,"[29] for history may
one day suggest that you stood on the side of righteousness.

Wisdom Saying #2: "Keep the faith"

African American elders who remember lynching and a culture of lynching invite younger generations who reside in a
land where "justice is merely incidental to law and order"[30] to
"put all their trust in God Almighty."[31] As they reflect on life in
the United States when domestic terror was an accepted practice, African American elders speak openly about their faith.
For many, such as Hannah White Allen, lynching "didn't stop
[them] from believing in God."[32] Rather, these elders make
a distinction between the oppressors' object of worship and

their own faith in the true and living God who sets captives free. As retired educator Mordessa Corbin states, "[Faith in God] was the only source of protection and strength that we had and we knew that."[33] For this reason, African American elders who remember lynching want future generations to know:

> Faith gave us strength to endure many of the wrongs that was and is being done to us. Our faith was the only thing that we had to sustain us. We have always had, blacks have always had strong faith and we have looked to a higher power—looked to the Lord for whatever we needed when we needed it because that was our only source and we know that today.[34]

This reliance on the divine is not to be equated with conformance to the status quo. Rather, these elders' faith is one forged from an active engagement in multiple sectors of society. Speaking from a broad spectrum of professional experiences, these elders speak of faith as a life-giving force. For example, when Reverence Clarence Kidd reflects on a correlation between lynching and faith in God, he wants future generations to know:

> [Lynching shaped my faith] because I knew that God was there. That's the only way that I could live through this stuff is that God was always there with me causing me to even receive sometimes what could be thought of as a blessing because many times I saw the whites treating others a different way and when they would come to me, they'd talk to me like I was a human being. I've seen that and I could recognize them and that was not because they were doing it—it was from beyond.[35]

Concurring with Kidd, Collier Parks wants younger generations who are coming of age in a neo-lynching culture to know he "believes that God was able to bring us through all of this if we only had faith in God—because we didn't have any power. The other race of people had all the power and we had to depend on God to see us through all of this."[36] However, I want to stress that it is essential that future generations understand that faith in God alone does not guarantee a reciprocal response of repentance from perpetrators of evil that can lead to an eradication of systems predicated on abuse. What Kidd and others want future generations to understand is that faith in God "is an attitude of trust."[37] Faith is not a panacea. Rather, an ability to trust in God demands a type of dexterity to read situations and people that enables persons of faith to respond in a manner that speaks to the collective situation of black life in the United States.

As long as one person questions whether black lives matter, African American elders who remember lynching want future generations to "seek and know the Lord, develop a strong faith, ask God to lead them, and know what Jesus said—the things that he did [they] can do and even greater things."[38] This is the good news a generation of elders wants to convey to a generation of young black persons who find themselves confronted with similar challenges of domestic terror. This proclamation to "be strong in the Lord and in the strength of the Lord's power"[39] is a call to active faith. It is in some regards a charge from the elders to current and future generations to be vigilant in their pursuit to name injustices for which persons charged to protect and serve are often exempt from being responsible and accountable.

These elders want current and future generations to identify for themselves christological accounts that portray a

Jesus who confronted the status quo and questioned exploit-
ative practices as they address simultaneously issues of complicity in which Jesus participated. What this suggests is that
perpetrators of injustice who also self-identify as Christians
have a responsibility to listen and to hear how their actions
are viewed as antithetical to a professed faith premised upon
love. It is this notion of a desire to meet people at their point
of need that causes me to conclude that African American
elders who lived through a season of orchestrated fear could
compel the church to consider its role in fostering environ-
ments where repentance and forgiveness are central to the
ongoing formation of persons who claim to be followers of
Jesus. At the very least, African American elders who remember lynching want future generations of black people to keep
the faith, attentive always to the interweaving of time past
and time present as indicators of a time yet to come. With
faith in God, these elders are "just hopeful that it will be even
better in the future."[40] In the meantime, these elders want to
encourage black people who are coming of age in a climate of
neo-lynching to remain unwavering in their quest for justice.

Wisdom Saying #3: "Learn all you can"

Connected closely to establishing goals and trusting in a
higher power is a desire for future generations to value learning. More than sixty years after the US Supreme Court's 1954
landmark decision in *Brown v. Board of Education*[41] to end
segregation in public schools, African Americans who remember lynching stress that education is "the strongest weapon
against segregation."[42] In response to this strong statement
about education as a tool to dismantle a system based on
white supremacy, Dr. George Hampton asserts, "If there's any
future for black folks in America, it's through education."[43]

With personal experiences of the fallacy of separate but equal policies, these elders "admonish all young people to get an education. Get as much as you can. Study history, learn as much as you can and by all means, don't forget to pray."[44]

At the same time, given the financial reality of student indebtedness, these elders realize that prayer alone is not sufficient. Thus, they stress that educating future generations must become a shared responsibility. Hampton, for instance, acknowledges that some parents may lack the financial resources to underwrite a child's college education. He also notes that some children may not be "smart enough to get a scholarship." What Hampton and others fail to address explicitly are systems that privilege legacy admissions, often extended to prospective students irrespective of intellectual ability. These elders also do not discuss a growing trend in college admissions whereby scholarships are offered to persons for whom financial need is irrelevant. As Hampton reflects on his own educational journey and his commitment to invest in his granddaughter's education, he shares, "As rough as things were for me trying to get through school on my own, I didn't want to see her have to do that."[45]

Like Hampton, Odell Carr is also a proponent of a collective financial approach to fund future generations' education. While she, unlike Hampton, is not a college graduate, Carr says,

> [I] can feel good to know that I helped my grandchildren and other children because now, I don't have any grandchildren in college. They've all finished and have good jobs and all that but I still help others so that they can get an education because I know that that's what it's going to take. . . . It takes education and I would just

> tell the kids that no matter how hard it is, just keep on
> trying, keep pushing, keep pushing until you get all the
> education you can—you can't get too much.[46]

With a keen awareness that reading is fundamental and that
learning is essential in all aspects of life, African American
elders want future generations to

> further [their] education, because to drive a garbage
> truck, [they've] got to have education, to empty some-
> body else's garbage, [they've] got to have education. So
> now ain't nothing out there gonna be given to [them]
> free. Go to school and try to get some education,
> because education now is free.[47]

While public school may in concept be viewed as free, alloca-
tion of tax dollars suggests that equality and quality are not
easily achieved through legislative initiatives. Nevertheless,
African American elders want future generations to know
"[they're] gonna need [their] education, because otherwise,
[they] ain't gonna survive."[48]

For this reason, African American elders recognize a
need to work to dismantle systems designed to control the
production of knowledge while simultaneously encouraging
future generations to

> get the best education you can get. Stay with God in
> prayer so that you will be able to compete and maybe
> you can be fairly rewarded for your education, for your
> knowledge, for your ability, for the skills you have, for
> the degrees you have—maybe you can be fairly rewarded
> for that. But you need to get the best education you can

get. You don't need to waste time playing around. The day is going to come where a bachelor's degree with me in my era was tops. But there's going to come a time when the master's degree is going to be. It's now where young folks could get jobs and didn't have a high school education. We're getting past that and you have to have a degree. So the day is going to come when these young folks are going to have a master's degree in some specialty, especially technology.[49]

While African American elders who remember lynching value formal education, an emphasis on higher education is not to be equated as a standard to which all future generations must subscribe. What the elders most want to communicate is the maxim that knowledge is the one thing no one can take from any person. It is this understanding of learning as a process of formation that retired pastor and civil rights activist William Randolph views as connected intricately to a system of values. Randolph suggests, "If somehow we could educate family to understand that it's not the school that's responsible for teaching [our children] morals," then there is a possibility that future generations would become increasingly more "involved in education, involved in the church, volunteerism."[50]

For Randolph and others, it is imperative that future generations of black people understand the significance of their active participation in various arenas in which learning occurs. From the elders' point of view, they want future generations to realize that engagement in multiple sectors of society is "not always what you can get out of it, money wise, but to get the experience of knowing how people have to go through certain things in order to just have somebody there that will listen, given them a hug, and say, 'You can make it. You can do it.'"[51] This valuing of experiential learning points to ways in which African American elders celebrate individuals' accomplishments while also reminding future generations to be attentive to recognize that education is never a solo endeavor.

As African American elders reflect on their educational experiences and life lessons, they urge future generations to remember

> every victory we think we have won, we just have to keep winning it over and over. Nothing stays won. We can't afford the luxury of overdosing on our successes, thinking that we have arrived. We need each other. Not enough to be individually involved, individually upset, but we need to be a part of a community. We need each other. And that's our hope, laboring together as a community, . . . overcoming it by the grace of God.[52]

More than six decades since the highest court in the United States issued a ruling to desegregate schools with all deliberate speed, African American elders who remember lynching encourage future generations of black people not to "waste your time by not getting a complete education because that's the key—that's the key. You need it."[53] As they remember a time when African American college graduates had limited professional opportunities, these elders want future generations to cultivate a desire for learning that includes, but is not restricted to, traditional sites of education. In each encounter, these elders want future generations to learn all they can and to consider how to apply their knowledge strategically as they continue to navigate life in a neo-lynching culture.

Wisdom Saying #4: "Learn to forgive"

Central to African American elders' insights about life is a desire that future generations learn to forgive. For Katherine Clark Fletcher, who shared vivid recollections about two lynchings that occurred in the St. Joseph, Missouri, area, forgiveness is something she "learned early in life." After her parents died, and subsequent to her adoption and relocation from Colorado to Missouri, Fletcher had to come to terms with her aunt's meanness. Although she never discovered the cause of her aunt's behavior, Fletcher explains, "[I] always had a feeling there was something that had happened to her. I was able to forgive her completely." Fletcher wants future generations to understand that an intentional decision to forgive is not synonymous with forgetting. As her narrative makes clear, to forgive should not be misinterpreted as "making excuses for people." Instead, Fletcher wants future generations to be able to "look beyond, behind the behavior for causes."[54] From a situational analysis perspective, Fletcher wants future generations to be able to envision forgiveness as a process through which an individual exercises agency to come to terms with circumstances and determines what steps are essential to being a person of integrity.

In her case, Fletcher says, "[I] learned to forgive so that I don't have to carry around anger or disappointment or what have you. That's not a part of the baggage that I carry around. When I go to sleep at night, I'm not worrying about what someone has done to me or what I've done to somebody." It is this sense of being at peace that African American elders who remember lynching want future generations to experience. For young black people who find themselves on the vanguard of social issues, these elders speak across generations

to encourage them to "learn to forgive."[55] As future generations are compelled to confront systems that at times appear
impenetrable, African American elders advance an ethic of
forgiveness that requires an ongoing evaluation of where and
how energy is expended.

In these days of neo-lynching, these elders do not want
young black people to remain silent. They want future generations of black people to know that a decision to forgive will
empower them both to name evil unambiguously in all its
complexity and to offer a comprehensive solution developed
to address the magnitude of contemporary issues forged in
a national identity that benefits from selective forgetfulness.
African American elders who came of age during a time when
silence was often employed as a strategy of resistance want
future generations of black people to learn how to forgive in
order to minimize a distortion of truth. As the world observes
the United States' inability to live into its own declaration of
inalienable rights that all people are created equal, African
American elders encourage future generations of black people
and those aligned with them to learn to forgive and never forget "the contributions, the sacrifices, the wisdom, the faith"[56]
of previous generations.

A Concluding Reflection

African American elders' lynching narratives are primary
sources for historical reconstruction that extend beyond the
narrators' remembrances and the relevance of their accounts
for a particular community at a specific point in time. African American women and men who remember lynching want
future generations to "be honest in everything that [they]
do"[57] and "treat people fairly."[58] This ethic of veracity aligns
closely and is informed by an ethic of forgiveness. As such,

African American elders implore younger generations to adopt a set of core values that minimizes their potential to "sacrifice their beliefs and their integrity for the simple things in life."[59] Of utmost importance to these elders is that future generations "know who they are so that they can be true to themselves and refuse to yield to anything for popularity."[60] In a context where the value and significance of black lives is constantly subjected to scrutiny, African American elders who remember lynching

> say to each generation that the torch is passed to you and you dare not let it die, nor you dare not forget the shoulders on whom you stand. . . . We are to always be open-minded, to always seek justice for all people, especially when we see injustice being perpetrated. . . . And so I would say to the young people that we need to always remember that we're all in this boat together and that we can go much further if we row in the same direction.[61]

I am thankful that these oral histories offer ethical-theological insights into and a potential response to counter the deadly effects of a neo-lynching culture that is a current reality in the United States of America. Perhaps for such a time as now, as persons from multiple locales in the world contemplate the significance of black lives, we are encouraged to engage these elders' voices as primary sources for moral decision making. From these memories of lynching and a culture of lynching, African American elders ask that we think long and hard about strategies of resistance in a context where even today a look, a movement, a word can translate into death not only for an individual but also for his or her family.

Notes

Preface

1   A recording of Sherrod's speech is archived on the NAACP's
    website: http://www.naacp.org/news/entry/video_sherrod/
    (accessed December 24, 2015). For additional information,
    see Kam Williams, "Shirley Sherrod: Wronged Role Model
    Discusses Restoring Her Reputation; The 'Martin Luther King
    Awards Dinner' Interview," *Journal of Pan African Studies* 6,
    no. 9 (2014): 140; Pete Daniel, *Dispossession: Discrimination
    against African American Farmers in the Age of Civil Rights*
    (Chapel Hill: University of North Carolina Press, 2013),
    263–64.

1: Echoes of a Not So Distant Past

1   All participants signed and were provided a copy of the Saint
    Paul School of Theology's Information and Consent Form and
    the Baylor University Institute for Oral History's Oral History
    Deed of Gift Agreement.

2   A working hypothesis for the oral history project presumed that a recovery of accounts of African American memories of lynching and a culture of lynching would illustrate ways in which people of faith reimagined biblical principles, such as salvation and reconciliation, and how these understandings provide lessons that are applicable to the life of the church in the twenty-first century.

3   The four primary questions were: (1) Why do you think people do or do not talk about lynching and what it means? (2) Since you grew up in a time when lynching or the possibility of lynching was a part of society, how did this practice shape your understanding of justice and faith in God? (3) Why should lynching be of concern for the church in the twenty-first century? (4) With more than seventy-five years of life experience, what words of wisdom do you want to give to future generations?

4   Participants self-identified as the National Baptist Convention, USA, Inc.; Progressive National Baptist Convention Inc.; Southern Baptist; United Methodist; Roman Catholic; Presbyterian (USA); and Church of God in Christ.

5   The exhibit opened to the public on April 23, 2009. See Dorie Turner, "Alice Walker Exhibit Opens at Emory University," *Network Journal*, April 24, 2009, http://www.tnj.com/arts--entertainments/alice-walker-exhibit-opens-at-emory-university.

6   Martin O'Neal Collins, interview by Angela D. Sims, August 20, 2009, in Monroe, La., transcript, Baylor University Institute for Oral History, Waco, Tex., available online at http://digitalcollections.baylor.edu/cdm/ref/collection/buioh/id/6603.

7   St. Stephen Baptist Church members compiled three books to record the church's history: *One Hundred Years: Commemorative Souvenir Book 1903–2003*; *Symbols of Grace 1903–1973*; and *Meeting the Challenge of Change 1903–1963*.

8   *One Hundred Years*, 77.

9   See World Faith News archives, Carol J. Fouke, "NCCCUSA Dr. Mac Charles Jones Dies—Updated," http://www.wfn .org/1997/03/msg00064.html (accessed December 22, 2015).

10 For additional information about Reverend Dr. Mac Charles Jones, see *One Hundred Years*, 76–84. Also see the following for information about Jones' faith-informed activism: Sam E. Mann, "Not an Unfinished Symphony," *Sojourners*, May–June 1997; Robert McG. Thomas Jr., "Mac Jones, 47, Who Aided Burned Churches," *New York Times*, March 10, 1997; Worldwide Faith News archives, "WCC Head on Mac Charles Jones Death," http://archive.wfn.org/1997/03/msg00061 .html (accessed December 22, 2015).

11 Erik Stafford's "There Was a Hanging Tree in Westport" is no longer available on myspace.com, and the author, per a January 16, 2015, e-mail, is unable to retrieve the article. While a walking tour conducted by the author did not yield additional information by which to verify his sources, Sherilyn Iliff's *On the Courthouse Lawn: Confronting the Legacy of Lynching in the Twenty-First Century* (Boston: Beacon, 2007) presents evidence to support trees as sites of killing fields. Professional photographer Joshua Kristal recently completed a project to document hanging trees as a visual socio-historical memorial; see "Show at the Society for Domestic Museology," blog entry by Joshua Kristal, October 29, 2014, https://machup icchuthis.wordpress.com/2014/10/29/show-at-the-society -for-domestic-museology/ (accessed December 22, 2015). Also see Harriet C. Frazier, *Lynchings in Missouri, 1803–1981* (Jefferson, N.C.: McFarland, 2009).

12 For additional information, see the list of "Louisiana Lynchings 1878–1946" compiled by Michael J. Pfeifer and included in the June 13, 2005, Congressional Record: http://www.gpo.gov/ fdsys/pkg/CREC-2005-06-13/html/CREC-2005-06-13-pt1 -PgS6364-3.htm (accessed December 22, 2015); Emily Lane, "Lynchings Map Shows 540 Victims in Louisiana between 1877–1950, *New York Times* Reports," NOLA.com, http://

www.nola.com/news/baton-rouge/index.ssf/2015/02/lynch ings_louisiana_report.html; "A Closer Look at Louisiana's Lynchings," IND, February 12, 2015, http://theind.com/ article-20224-a-closer-look-at-louisiana's-lynchings.html.

13 Hazel Peoples Thompson, interview by Angela D. Sims, January 15, 2010, in Oakland, Calif., transcript, Baylor University Institute for Oral History, Waco, Tex., available online at http://digitalcollections.baylor.edu/cdm/ref/collection/ buioh/id/6630.

14 A direct reference to her husband, Leon Thompson.

15 Thompson, interview by Sims, January 15, 2010.

16 African American newspapers are archived at the Moorland-Spingarn Library at Howard University in Washington, D.C.: http://www.coas.howard.edu/msrc/treasures_african -american-newspapers.html (accessed December 22, 2015).

17 Thompson, interview by Sims, January 15, 2010.

18 Alice Walker, *The Same River Twice: Honoring the Difficult; A Meditation on Life, Spirit, Art and the Making of the Film "The Color Purple" Ten Years Later* (New York: Scribner, 1996), 50.

19 For a historical overview of Victoria, Texas, see "Victoria County," Texas State Historical Association, http://www .tshaonline.org/handbook/online/articles/hcv03 (accessed December 22, 2015).

20 Ireland Hill, interview by Angela D. Sims, January 13, 2010, in Oakland, Calif., transcript, Baylor University Institute for Oral History, Waco, Tex., available online at http://digital collections.baylor.edu/cdm/ref/collection/buioh/id/7023.

21 Philip Dray, *At the Hands of Persons Unknown: The Lynching of Black America* (New York: Modern Library, 2002).

22 About two years after Hill relocated to California, Victoria's population of twelve thousand included—according to a June 29, 1942, *Life* article—approximately two dozen millionaires. See "Victoria, Texas: The Air Forces Come to a Rich Texas

Cattle Town Whose Worries Turned into Warm Welcome." *Life,* June 29, 1942, 56–61.

23 Hill, interview by Sims, January 13, 2010.

24 Parenthetical note added as emphasis since it is impossible to know the exact number of lynchings for any given period.

25 Arthur F. Raper, *The Tragedy of Lynching* (Mineola, N.Y.: Dover, 2003), 28.

26 See *Chicago Record's* March 14, 1901, article reprinted in Ralph Ginzburg, *100 Years of Lynchings* (Baltimore, Md.: Black Classic, 1962, 1988), 38.

27 See *Chicago Record-Herald* article reprinted in Ginzburg, *100 Years of Lynchings,* 45–46.

28 See *Chicago Record-Herald* article reprinted in Ginzburg, *100 Years of Lynchings,* 61.

29 See *Montgomery Advertiser* article and editorial from the *Literary Digest* (New York) in Ginzburg, *100 Years of Lynchings,* 70–71.

30 See *Atlanta Constitution* article reprinted in Ginzburg, *100 Years of Lynchings,* 80. Of particular note is the observation that "Rucker was the second negro to die for the murder of Mrs. Williams. . . . Friday a mob hanged a negro named Andrew Williams for the same crime. Williams' innocence has since been established."

31 See *Birmingham News's* February 27, 1913, article reprinted in Ginzburg, *100 Years of Lynchings,* 80–81.

32 See *Montgomery Advertiser* article reprinted in Ginzburg, *100 Years of Lynchings,* 81.

33 See *Boston Guardian's* April 30, 1914, article reprinted in Ginzburg, *100 Years of Lynchings,* 45–46.

34 See *Galveston News's* (Tex.) October 15, 1914, article reprinted in Ginzburg, *100 Years of Lynchings,* 92.

35 See *New York World's* May 16, 1916, article reprinted in Ginzburg, *100 Years of Lynchings,* 103.

36 See *Chicago Defender's* October 13, 1917, article reprinted in Ginzburg, *100 Years of Lynchings,* 113–14.

37 See various articles reprinted in Ginzburg, *100 Years of Lynchings*, 138–40, 153, 155, 157–58, 161–64, 166–68.

38 Raper, *Tragedy of Lynching*, 3. Also see *Columbus Enquirer-Sun*'s (Georgia) May 10 and 11, 1930, articles; *New York Sun*'s May 10, 1930, article; and *Chicago Defender*'s May 17, 1930, article reprinted in Ginzburg, *100 Years of Lynchings*, 181–85.

39 Edward H. Phillips, "The Sherman Courthouse Riot of 1930," *East Texas Historical Journal* 25, no. 2 (1987): 12–15. For additional details about the May 10, 1930, mob in Sherman, Texas, see the reprint of *Columbus Enquirer-Sun*'s (Georgia) May 10 and 11, 1930 articles; *New York Sun*'s May 10, 1930, article; and *Chicago Defender*'s May 17, 1930, article in Ginzburg, *100 Years of Lynchings*, 181–85.

40 "Lynching," Texas State Historical Association, http://www.tshaonline.org/handbook/online/articles/jgl01 (accessed December 22, 2015).

41 "Lynching," Texas State Historical Association.

42 For additional information, see David Campbell, "Horrific Blindness: Images of Death in Contemporary Media," *Journal for Cultural Research* 8, no. 1 (2004): 55–74; Josh Rosenblatt, "Long Road Out of Jasper: A Documentary Chronicles James Byrd's Life and Tragic Death," *Texas Observer*, July 25, 2013, http://www.texasobserver.org/long-road-out-of-jasper/; "James Byrd's Killer: 'I'd do it all over again,'" KHOU.com, September 20, 2011, http://www.khou.com/story/news/2014/07/17/11531380/.

43 Walker, *Same River Twice*, 50.

44 Jessie Eva Manley Dean, interview by Angela D. Sims, February 13, 2010, in Norfolk, Va., transcript, Baylor University Institute for Oral History, Waco, Tex., available online at http://digitalcollections.baylor.edu/cdm/ref/collection/buioh/id/6607.

45 For one summary of lynchings in Virginia, see Ginzburg, *100 Years of Lynchings*, 270. While Ginzburg reports the last lynching in the Commonwealth of Virginia as that of an

"unknown Negro in Hopeful on December 9, 1915," other sources, such as the *Encyclopedia Virginia*, indicate lynchings occurred after that date: i.e., the November 30, 1927, lynching of Leonard Woods by a "mob estimated at three hundred to four hundred people on a platform straddling the Virginia-Kentucky border." Douglas Smith, "Anti-lynching Law of 1928," *Encyclopedia Virginia*, http://www.encyclopedia virginia.org/Antilynching_Law_of_1928#start_entry.

46 See Kenneth S. Greenberg, ed., *The Confessions of Nat Turner: And Related Documents* (New York: Bedford/St. Martin's, 1996); Scot French, *The Rebellious Slave: Nat Turner in American History* (Boston: Houghton Mifflin, 2004); Kenneth S. Greenberg, ed., *Nat Turner: A Slave Rebellion in History and Memory* (New York: Oxford University Press, 2003); Mary Kemp Davis, *Nat Turner before the Bar of Judgment: Fictional Treatments of the Southampton Slave Insurrection* (Baton Rouge: Louisiana State University Press, 1999).

47 "On March 14, 1928, Governor Harry F. Byrd, Sr. signed into law the nation's strictest anti-lynching measure and the first that directly termed lynching a state crime. No white person was ever convicted under the statute for committing crimes against an African American. Instead, Virginia's landmark anti-lynching law was used only to punish whites for crimes against other whites." Smith, "Anti-lynching Law of 1928," *Encyclopedia Virginia*.

48 J. Douglas Smith, *Managing White Supremacy: Race, Politics, and Citizenship in Jim Crow Virginia* (Chapel Hill: University of North Carolina Press, 2002), 155.

49 Smith, *Managing White Supremacy*; and Alexander Leidholdt, *Standing before the Shouting Mob: Lenoir Chambers and Virginia's Massive Resistance to Public-School Integration* (Tuscaloosa: University of Alabama Press, 1997). These two texts provide a descriptive analysis of Virginia's 1928 anti-lynching law.

50   Nansemond County, originally known as Upper Norfolk County, merged with the city of Suffolk, Virginia, in 1974. For additional information, see John Dunn Bragg, *The History of Nansemond County, Virginia* (1907), digitized by the Library of Congress at http://www.archive.org/details/history ofnansemoooodunn (accessed December 22, 2015); George MacLaren Brydon, *Virginia's Mother Church and the Political Conditions under Which It Grew* (Richmond: Virginia Historical Society, 1947), iii.

51   See "Nat Turner's Rebellion," PBS, http://www.pbs.org/wgbh/ aia/part3/3p1518.html; "The Confessions of Nat Turner," PBS, http://www.pbs.org/wgbh/aia/part3/3h500t.html; and "The *Richmond Enquirer* on Nat Turner's Rebellion (Virginia, August 30, 1831)," PBS, http://www.pbs.org/wgbh/aia/ part3/3h499t.html.

52   Franklin—located in the southeastern, or Tidewater, section of Virginia—is forty miles west of Norfolk and nine miles north of the North Carolina border. Located at the head of the navigable portion of the Blackwater River, Franklin, situated on the eastern edge of Southampton County, has always been a center of trade and transportation for the surrounding countryside. See "Visitors," City of Franklin, Virginia, http://www .franklinva.com/index.php?option=com_content&view= article&id=47&Itemid=188 (accessed December 22, 2015).

53   Dean, interview by Sims, February 13, 2010.

54   Lucille Otis Jones, interview by Angela D. Sims, December 28, 2009, in Lake Charles, La., transcript, Baylor University Institute for Oral History, Waco, Tex., available online at http:// digitalcollections.baylor.edu/cdm/ref/collection/buioh/ id/7024.

55   Angela D. Sims, *Ethical Complications of Lynching: Ida B. Wells's Interrogation of American Terror* (New York: Palgrave Macmillan, 2010), 30.

56   The Knights of the White Camelia was established at Franklin, Louisiana, on May 22, 1867, by Alcibiades DeBlanc—a veteran

of St. Martinville's antebellum vigilante committee and a former Confederate officer who, at the end of the Civil War, had used his military authority to reestablish antebellum controls over freedmen—and Daniel Dennett, editor of the Franklin Planters' Banner and perhaps the most prominent journalist in rural south Louisiana. See Carl A. Brasseaux, *Acadian to Cajun: Transformation of a People, 1803–1877* (Jackson: University Press of Mississippi, 1992), 136.

57 Brasseaux, *Acadian to Cajun*, 137.

58 Brasseaux, *Acadian to Cajun*, 137. "The area of Louisiana, now known as Acadiana, comprised about 22 parishes. It forms a triangle from Lake Charles at the west to Grand Isle at the east, with Pointe Coupee at the apex. The Acadians were the largest group to settle in this area from 1765 to 1785. Although other nationalities were there, the Acadian culture was dominant in many places. When bits and pieces of these other cultures were added to the Acadians, a variation of the Acadian culture was created. These people, and this culture, became known as Cajun . . . a derivation of the word Acadian." "History of the Cajuns," Acadian-Cajun Genealogy and History, http://www.acadian-cajun.com/hiscaj1.htm (accessed December 22, 2015). The twenty-two Acadian parishes are Acadia, Ascension, Assumption, Avoyelles, Calcasieu, Cameron, Evangeline, Iberia, Iberville, Jefferson Davis, Lafayette, Lafourche, Point Coupée, St. Charles, St. James, St. John the Baptist, St. Landry, St. Martin, St. Mary, Terrebonne, Vermilion, and W. Baton Rouge. See "Maps: Louisiana Parishes, Tourist Regions & Acadiana Parishes," http://www.thecajuns.com/parishes.htm (accessed December 22, 2015).

59 Brasseaux, *Acadian to Cajun*, 141.

60 For additional information on this regional Klan group, with a presence primarily in Louisiana, Arkansas, Texas, and Oklahoma, see "Ku Klux Klan Extremism in America," ADL, http://www.adl.org/learn/ext_us/kkk/changes.asp?LEARN

_Cat=Extremism&LEARN_SubCat=Extremism_in_America
&xpicked=4&item=kkk (accessed December 22, 2015).

61 For information on this organization founded in Louisiana in
1956, see Stephen E. Atkins, *Encyclopedia of Modern Worldwide Extremists and Extremist Groups* (Westport, Conn.:
Greenwood, 2004).

62 For information on this group with chapters in Florida and
Louisiana, see "Extremism in American," ADL, http://archive
.adl.org/learn/ext_us/aryan_nations.html (accessed December 22, 2015).

63 For information on this group reported to operate only in the
state of Florida, see Arnold S. Rice, *The Ku Klux Klan in American Politics* (Washington, D.C.: Public Affairs Press, 1962).

64 In the early nineteenth century, Franklin became an interior sugar port, with the area's sugarcane planters among the
South's wealthiest agriculturists. For additional information,
see "About the City of Franklin," City of Franklin, http://www
.franklin-la.com/about.php (accessed December 22, 2015).

65 Jones, interview by Sims, December 28, 2009.

66 Laura Wexler, *Fire in a Canebrake: The Last Mass Lynching
in America* (New York: Scribner, 2003).

67 Howard Thurman, "The Negro Spiritual Speaks of Life and
Death," in *African American Religious Thought: An Anthol-
ogy*, ed. Cornel West and Eddie S. Glaude Jr. (Louisville, Ky.:
Westminster John Knox, 2003), 29.

68 Addie S. Bolton, interview by Angela D. Sims, August 13, 2009,
in Winnsboro, La., transcript, Baylor University Institute for
Oral History, Waco, Tex., available online at http://digital
collections.baylor.edu/cdm/ref/collection/buioh/id/6598.

69 Bolton, interview by Sims, August 13, 2009.

70 Michael J. Pfeifer, *The Roots of Rough Justice: Origins of
American Lynching* (Urbana: University of Illinois Press,
2011), 83.

71 In her 1895 publication, *A Red Record: Tabulated Statistics
and Alleged Causes of Lynchings in the United States*, Ida B.

Wells wrote, "From the record published in the Chicago Tri-
bune, January 1, 1894, the following computation of lynching statistics is made referring only to the colored victims of
Lynch Law during the year 1893: . . . Poisoning Wells Aug. 18,
two unknown negroes, Franklin Parish, La." Wells-Barnett,
Selected Works of Ida B. Wells-Barnett, compiled with an
introduction by Trudier Harris (New York: Oxford University
Press, 1991), 150 and 154.

72 Raper, *Tragedy of Lynching.* In "Musings on the Louisiana
Delta from a Native Son," Pete Gregory recounts that his
"grandfather said they went to school right after the Civil War,
but they had a lynching in Winnsboro, and whites came to the
school to get the boys to go see the lynching. The schoolteacher
was from the north and she told him, 'If they go to the lynching, they can't come back to school.' 'Well, good,' they said and
then took them to the lynching and never let them go back to
school." See "Musings on the Louisiana Delta from a Native
Son," Folklife in Louisiana, http://www.louisianafolklife.org/
LT/Articles_Essays/DeltaGregory.html (accessed December
22, 2015).

73 See Marcia Riggs' *Awake, Arise, and ACT: A Womanist
Call for Black Liberation* (Cleveland: Pilgrim, 1994); Evangeline Holland, "Lifting as We Climb: The Women's Club
Movement," Edwardian Promenade, http://www.edwardian
promenade.com/african-american/lifting-as-we-climb/
(accessed December 22, 2015).

74 Many of these retired educators are active members of their
sororities' and fraternities' graduate chapters.

75 See Will Sentel, "Report: Louisiana Public Education Ranked
in Bottom 10 in Country, up Slightly from Past Year," *Acadiana Advocate,* January 8, 2015, http://theadvocate.com/
news/acadiana/11285179-123/report-louisiana-public
-education-ranked.

76 Mordessa Corbin, interview by Angela D. Sims, August
13, 2009, in Winnsboro, La., transcript, Baylor University

Institute for Oral History, Waco, Tex., available online at http://digitalcollections.baylor.edu/cdm/ref/collection/buioh/id/6598.

77 Corbin, interview by Sims, August 13, 2009.

78 For information on the March 7, 1965, act of legally sanctioned assault on peaceful demonstrators in Selma, Alabama, see Barbara Harris Combs, *From Selma to Montgomery: The Long March to Freedom* (New York: Routledge, 2014); Bernard Lafayette Jr. and Kathryn Lee Johnson, *In Peace and Freedom: My Journey in Selma* (Lexington: University Press of Kentucky, 2013); Christopher A. Varlack, "Reflections of the 1965 Freedom March from Selma to Montgomery, Alabama," *Journal of Pan African Studies (Online)* 6, no. 10 (2014).

79 "Justice Department Announces Findings of Two Civil Rights Investigations in Ferguson, Missouri," Department of Justice, http://www.justice.gov/opa/pr/justice-department-announces-findings-two-civil-rights-investigations-ferguson-missouri (accessed December 22, 2015).

80 Corbin, interview by Sims, August 13, 2009.

81 "Police Killed More than 100 Unarmed Black People in 2015, Mapping Police Violence," http://mappingpolice violence.org/unarmed/ (accessed December 22, 2015); Aamer Madhani, "Timeline: Dozens of unarmed African Americans killed since Ferguson," *USA Today*, August 8, 2015, http://www.usatoday.com/story/news/2015/08/09/timeline-dozens-unarmed-african-americans-killed-since-ferguson/31375795/.

82 Corbin, interview by Sims, August 13, 2009.

83 Corbin, interview by Sims, August 13, 2009.

84 Joseph Purvis, interview by Angela D. Sims, February 13, 2010, in Norfolk, Va., transcript, Baylor University Institute for Oral History, Waco, Tex., available online at http://digital collections.baylor.edu/cdm/ref/collection/buioh/id/6622.

85 Collins, interview by Sims, August 20, 2009.

86 Ian Tuttle, "The Injustice the DOJ Uncovered in Ferguson Wasn't Racism," *National Review*, March 6, 2015, http://www.nationalreview.com/article/415041/injustice -doj-uncovered-ferguson-wasnt-racism-ian-tuttle.

87 Tuttle, "Injustice."

88 On July 17, 2014, Eric Garner stated repeatedly, "I can't breathe," as New York City police officers strangled him to death for allegedly selling loose cigarettes. Garner's last words convey the gravity of what is at stake, and we are compelled to give voice to inhumane practices. Meena Krishnamurthy notes, "In an attempt to bring greater awareness and to motivate further action, there have also been media drives through social networking platforms such as Facebook and Twitter with the tag #Blacklivesmatter and #ICantBreathe" (Krishnamurthy, "(White) Tyranny and the Democratic Value of Distrust," *Monist* 98, no. 4 [2015]: 391–406). For comments on the significance of "I can't breathe," see Elahe Izadi, "'I can't breathe.' Eric Garner's Last Words Are 2014's Most Notable Quote, according to a Yale Librarian," *Washington Post*, December 9, 2014, https://www.washingtonpost.com/news/ post-nation/wp/2014/12/09/i-cant-breathe-eric-garners -last-words-are-2014s-most-notable-quote-according-to-yale -librarian/; "Eric Garner: Why #ICantBreathe Is Trending," BBC, December 4, 2014, http://www.bbc.co.uk/newsbeat/ article/30326891/eric-garner-why-icantbreathe-is-trending.

89 Nims Edward Gay Jr., interview by Angela D. Sims, September 4, 2009, in Birmingham, Ala., transcript, Baylor University Institute for Oral History, Waco, Tex., available online at http://digitalcollections.baylor.edu/cdm/ref/collection/ buioh/id/6618.

90 Gwendolyn Elaine Brown Hill, interview by Angela D. Sims, September 17, 2009, in Dallas, Tex., transcript, Baylor University Institute for Oral History, Waco, Tex., available online at http://digitalcollections.baylor.edu/cdm/ref/collection/ buioh/id/7016.

91 Junius Warren Nottingham, interview by Angela D. Sims, August 26, 2009, in Philadelphia, Penn., transcript, Baylor University Institute for Oral History, Waco, Tex., available online at http://digitalcollections.baylor.edu/cdm/ref/collection/buioh/id/6620.

92 Bozie Mae Walker, interview by Angela D. Sims, March 5, 2010, in Oklahoma City, Okla., transcript, Baylor University Institute for Oral History, Waco, Tex., available online at http://digitalcollections.baylor.edu/cdm/ref/collection/buioh/id/7026.

93 Wallace Hartsfield Sr., interview by Angela D. Sims, July 31, 2009, in Kansas City, Mo., transcript, Baylor University Institute for Oral History, Waco, Tex., available online at http://digitalcollections.baylor.edu/cdm/ref/collection/buioh/id/6619.

2: Courageous Truth Telling

1 For the 1894 speech Frederick Douglass delivered at Metropolitan African Methodist Episcopal Church in Washington, D.C., see http://teachingamericanhistory.org/library/document/lessons-of-the-hour-excerpt/ (accessed December 22, 2015).

2 Leonard Pitts Jr., "Commentary: Don't Let Beck, Barbour Rewrite African-Americans' Story," *McClatchy*, January 7, 2011, http://www.mcclatchydc.com/2011/01/07/106232/commentary-dont-let-beck-barbour.html.

3 References to shadows cast by lynching trees are discussed by scholars such as James H. Cone, *The Cross and the Lynching Tree* (Maryknoll, N.Y.: Orbis, 2011); Anne P. Rice, ed., *Witnessing Lynching: American Writers Respond* (New Brunswick, N.J.: Rutgers University Press, 2003).

4 For positions on this act of aggression against the United States, see Brian Michael Jenkins and John Paul Godges, eds., *The Long Shadow of 9/11: America's Response to Terrorism*

(Santa Monica, Calif.: Rand, 2011); Mark Lewis Taylor, *Religion, Politics, and the Christian Right: Post-9/11 Powers and American Empire* (Minneapolis: Fortress, 2005); Samantha Hauptman, *The Criminalization of Immigration: The Post 9/11 Moral Panic* (El Paso, Tex.: LFB Scholarly, 2013).

5   James Edmund Clark, interview by Angela D. Sims, November 24, 2009, in Hillside, N.J., transcript, Baylor University Institute for Oral History, Waco, Tex., available online at http:// digitalcollections.baylor.edu/cdm/ref/collection/buioh/ id/6601; Nottingham, interview by Sims, August 26, 2009; Sarah L. Hardimon, interview by Angela D. Sims, March 4, 2010, in Oklahoma City, Okla., transcript, Baylor University Institute for Oral History, Waco, Tex., available online at   http://digitalcollections.baylor.edu/cdm/ref/collection/ buioh/id/7022; Jones, interview by Sims, December 28, 2009; Walker, interview by Sims, March 5, 2010; L. P. Lewis, interview by Angela D. Sims, January 13, 2010, in Oakland, Calif., transcript, Baylor University Institute for Oral History, Waco, Tex., available online at http://digitalcollections.baylor.edu/ cdm/ref/collection/buioh/id/7023; Ora Morgan, interview by Angela D. Sims, July 14, 2009, in Woodbridge, Va., transcript, Baylor University Institute for Oral History, Waco, Tex., available online at http://digitalcollections.baylor.edu/cdm/ref/ collection/buioh/id/6642; Katherine Louise Clark Fletcher, interview by Angela D. Sims, August 31, 2009, in Omaha, Neb., transcript, Baylor University Institute for Oral History, Waco, Tex., available online at http://digitalcollections .baylor.edu/cdm/ref/collection/buioh/id/6616.

6   Here I refer to Katie Geneva Cannon's application of archaeological practices as a theological-ethical approach to reading texts as detailed in her essay "Unearthing Ethical Treasures: The Intrusive Markers of Social Class," in Katie Geneva Cannon, Emilie M. Townes, and Angela D. Sims, ed., *Womanist Theological Ethics: A Reader* (Louisville, Ky.: Westminster John Knox, 2011).

7   Lewis, interview by Sims, January 13, 2010.

8   Leola Johnson Arnold, interview by Angela D. Sims, January 14, 2010, in Oakland, Calif., transcript, Baylor University Institute for Oral History, Waco, Tex., available online at http://digitalcollections.baylor.edu/cdm/ref/collection/buioh/id/6595.

9   Clarence Walter Kidd, interview by Angela D. Sims, August 18, 2009, in Benton, La., transcript, Baylor University Institute for Oral History, Waco, Tex., available online at http://digital-collections.baylor.edu/cdm/ref/collection/buioh/id/6612.

10   C. W. Kidd, interview by Sims, August 18, 2009.

11   Willie Matthew Thomas, interview by Angela D. Sims, September 4, 2009, in Birmingham, Ala., transcript, Baylor University Institute for Oral History, Waco, Tex., available online at http://digitalcollections.baylor.edu/cdm/ref/collection/buioh/id/6629.

12   Rosalie Joseph, interview by Angela D. Sims, January 16, 2010, in Oakland, Calif., transcript, Baylor University Institute for Oral History, Waco, Tex., available online at http://digital collections.baylor.edu/cdm/ref/collection/buioh/id/7025.

13   Thomas, interview by Sims, September 4, 2009.

14   "Tuscaloosa, Alabama Negro Lynching . . . ," http://www.rarenewspapers.com/view/569869 (accessed December 22, 2015). While Thomas' personal experience with a lynch mob was averted, this was not the case for others as documented in these known accounts of lynchings in Alabama in the early 1930s. See, for instance, "Lynching in Alabama," PBS, http://www.pbs.org/wgbh/amex/scottsboro/sfeature/sf_lynching.html; B. J. Hollars, "Thirteen Loops: Race, Violence, and the Last Lynching in America" (MFA thesis, University of Alabama, 2010); Alfred L. Brophy, "'Cold Legal Points into Points of Flame': Karl Llewellyn Attacks Lynching," UNC Legal Studies Research Paper No. 2619895, June 17, 2015. For information about the Scottsboro Boys, see Dan T. Carter, *Scottsboro: A Tragedy of the American South* (Baton Rouge: Louisiana

State University Press, 2007); and James Goodman, *Stories of Scottsboro* (New York: First Vintage Books, 1995).

15   For information on Ku Klux Klan titles, see Annie Cooper Burton, *The Ku Klux Klan* (Los Angeles: W. T. Potter, 1916).

16   Thomas, interview by Sims, September 4, 2009.

17   I benefit tremendously from Emilie M. Townes' work on memory and a human capacity to confront evil and Michel-Rolph Trouillot's work on production of historical narratives. See their respective books, *Womanist Ethics and the Cultural Production of Evil* (New York: Palgrave, 2006); and *Silencing the Past: Power and the Production of History*, 2nd ed. (Boston: Beacon, 2015).

18   See Clifford Geertz, *The Interpretation of Cultures* (New York: Basic Books, 1973).

19   See Tim Walker, "Don't Know Much about History," National Education Association, http://www.nea.org/home/39060 .htm (accessed December 22, 2015).

20   Hardimon, interview by Sims, March 4, 2010.

21   Hartsfield, interview by Sims, July 31, 2009.

22   Fletcher, interview by Sims, August 31, 2009.

23   Fletcher, interview by Sims, August 31, 2009.

24   Hannah White Allen, interview by Angela D. Sims, March 5, 2010, in Oklahoma City, Okla., transcript, Baylor University Institute for Oral History, Waco, Tex., available online at http://digitalcollections.baylor.edu/cdm/ref/collection/ buioh/id/6593.

25   Long-term effects of preemptive strikes have, since the 2003 Iraqi occupation and simultaneous military engagement in Afghanistan and other undisclosed locales around the globe, been a topic of discussion by politicians, military personnel, journalists, academics, activists, clergy, and other concerned citizens. Although there is an unprecedented number of documented suicides, brain injuries, and dismemberment, it may be years before we can determine what effect extended tours of duty in countries ravaged by almost constant air and

ground warfare will have on veterans and civilian contractors as well as their families, friends, and communities, not to mention the many children and adults who are now left to rebuild their countries in the midst of mass devastation. We can only hope that the "keeping of the records" will comprise multiple perspectives.

26 Douglas Kellner, "Preemptive Strikes and the War on Iraq: A Critique of Bush Administration Unilateralism and Militarism," *New Political Science* 26, no. 3 (2004): 417–40.

27 When we consider that an improvised explosive device (IED), "also known as a roadside bomb, is a homemade bomb constructed and deployed in ways other than for use in conventional military action," it is quite possible that some might want to dismiss any correlation between the effects of these weapons (that "are [were] the number one cause of fatalities and injuries to US troops in Afghanistan") and lynching. At the same time, there may be a tendency to focus exclusively on "the enemy" and not contend with the causality of this action. Whether we shift full responsibility to the Taliban (or any other group) and their allies or acknowledge our national complicity in this deadly *war on terror*, African American elders who remember lynching remind us that the residual effects of an extra-legal form of violence, frequently exempt from due process of law, dictate that we think long and hard about non-visible wounds with which persons who are subjected to ever-present danger contend. To persevere in this climate requires an "ability to find the explosives before they blow up." For information on improvised explosive devices, see Arul Ramasamy, Stuart E. Harrisson, Jon C. Clasper, and Michael Stewart, "Injuries from Roadside Improvised Explosive Devices," *Journal of Trauma-Injury Infection & Critical Care* 65, no. 4 (October 2008): 910–14; "Improvised Explosive Devices (IEDs) / Booby Traps," http://www.global security.org/military/intro/ied.htm (accessed December 22, 2015); "Improvised Explosive Devices," NATO, http://

www.nato.int/cps/en/natohq/topics_72809.htm   (accessed December 22, 2015).

28 Dorothy Clark, interview by Angela D. Sims, November 24, 2009, in Hillside, N.J., transcript, Baylor University Institute for Oral History, Waco, Tex., available online at http://digital collections.baylor.edu/cdm/ref/collection/buioh/id/6601; Collins, interview by Sims, August 20, 2009; Fletcher, interview by Sims, August 31, 2009; Lettie Ruth Hunter, interview by Angela D. Sims, March 4, 2010, in Oklahoma City, Okla., transcript, Baylor University Institute for Oral History, Waco, Tex., available online at http://digitalcollections.baylor.edu/cdm/ref/collection/buioh/id/7018; Morgan, interview by Sims, July 14, 2009.

29 Collins, interview by Sims, August 20, 2009.

30 Collins, interview by Sims, August 20, 2009.

31 Freddie Foshee Cudjoe, interview by Angela D. Sims, March 4, 2010, in Oklahoma City, Okla., transcript, Baylor University Institute for Oral History, Waco, Tex., available online at   http://digitalcollections.baylor.edu/cdm/ref/collection/buioh/id/6605.

32 Cudjoe, interview by Sims, March 4, 2010.

33 Corbin, interview by Sims, August 13, 2009.

34 Lillian J. Blunt, interview by Angela D. Sims, August 13, 2009, in Winnsboro, La., transcript, Baylor University Institute for Oral History, Waco, Tex., available online at http://digital collections.baylor.edu/cdm/ref/collection/buioh/id/6598.

35 Collier Parks Jr., interview by Angela D. Sims, August 18, 2009, in Benton, La., transcript, Baylor University Institute for Oral History, Waco, Tex., available online at http://digital collections.baylor.edu/cdm/ref/collection/buioh/id/6612.

36 Cudjoe, interview by Sims, March 4, 2010.

37 For instance, an example graduate student Jonathan Butler's 2015 hunger strike to draw attention to longstanding and accepted racist practices at the University of Missouri's campus in Columbia. See Dana Ford, "Jonathan

Butler: Meet the Man Whose Hunger Strike Flipped the Script at Mizzou," CNN, November 10, 2015, http://www .cnn.com/2015/11/09/us/jonathan-butler-hunger -strike-missouri-profile/; Jon Schuppe, "Jonathan Butler: How a Grad Student's Hunger Strike Toppled a University President," NBC News, November 10, 2015, http://www .nbcnews.com/news/us-news/jonathan-butler-how -grad-students-hunger-strike-toppled-university-president -n460161; Koran Addo, "Activism Going Strong at Mizzou, Students Critical of Top Leadership," *St Louis Post-Dispatch (MO)*, November 6, 2015.

38 L. P. Lewis, interview by Angela D. Sims, January 13, 2010, in Oakland, Calif., transcript, Baylor University Institute for Oral History, Waco, Tex., available online at http://digital collections.baylor.edu/cdm/ref/collection/buioh/id/7023.

39 Fletcher, interview by Sims, August 31, 2009.

40 Fletcher, interview by Sims, August 31, 2009.

41 Hardimon, interview by Sims, March 4, 2010.

42 Hardimon, interview by Sims, March 4, 2010.

43 William S. Randolph, interview by Angela D. Sims, October 29, 2009, in Sumter, S.C., transcript, Baylor University Institute for Oral History, Waco, Tex., available online at http:// digitalcollections.baylor.edu/cdm/ref/collection/buioh/ id/6623.

44 Nazzaree Franklin, interview by Angela D. Sims, August 18, 2009, in Shreveport, La., transcript, Baylor University Institute for Oral History, Waco, Tex., available online at http:// digitalcollections.baylor.edu/cdm/ref/collection/buioh/ id/6611.

45 Lillian Marigny, interview by Angela D. Sims, March 5, 2010, in Oklahoma City, Okla., transcript, Baylor University Institute for Oral History, Waco, Tex., available online at http:// digitalcollections.baylor.edu/cdm/ref/collection/buioh/ id/6636.

46   Artie Lee Harris, interview by Angela D. Sims, July 16, 2009, in Occoquan, Va., transcript, Baylor University Institute for Oral History, Waco, Tex., available online at http://digital collections.baylor.edu/cdm/ref/collection/buioh/id/7015.

47   Donald Wayne Davis, interview by Angela D. Sims, March 4, 2010, in Oklahoma City, Okla., transcript, Baylor University Institute for Oral History, Waco, Tex., available online at http://digitalcollections.baylor.edu/cdm/ref/collection/buioh/id/6606.

48   Hartsfield, interview by Sims, July 31, 2009.

49   Davis, interview by Sims, March 4, 2010.

50   Frederick Douglass delivered this speech on January 9, 1894, at Metropolitan African Methodist Episcopal Church in Washington, D.C. See "Who We Are," Metropolitan African Methodist Episcopal Church, http://www.metropolitanamec.org/history.asp (accessed December 22, 2015).

51   Shirley Jean Jackson Johnson, interview by Angela D. Sims, February 23, 2011, in Dallas, Tex., transcript, Baylor University Institute for Oral History, Waco, Tex., available online at http://digitalcollections.baylor.edu/cdm/ref/collection/buioh/id/7020.

52   See Jon Cohen and Dan Balz, "Race Shapes Zimmerman Verdict Reaction," *Washington Post*, July 22, 2013, https://www.washingtonpost.com/politics/race-shapes-zimmerman-verdict-reaction/2013/07/22/3569662c-f2fc-11e2-8505-bf6f231e77b4_story.html; Andrew Cohen, "Law and Justice and George Zimmerman," *Atlantic*, July 13, 2013, http://www.theatlantic.com/national/archive/2013/07/law-and-justice-and-george-zimmerman/277772/.

53   James H. Cone, *The Cross and the Lynching Tree* (Maryknoll, N.Y.: Orbis, 2011). See also James H. Cone's November 23, 2007, interview with Bill Moyers at http://www.pbs.org/moyers/journal/11232007/watch.html (accessed December 22, 2015).

54   Alice Walker, *Living by the Word: Essays* (San Diego: Harcourt Brace, 1988), 62.

55   Walker, *Living by the Word*, 63.

56   Walker, *Living by the Word*, 63.

57   Alice Walker, *The Same River Twice: Honoring the Difficult; A Meditation on Life, Spirit, Art, and the Making of the Film "The Color Purple" Ten Years Later* (New York: Scribner, 1996), 50; quoted in Angela D. Sims, *Ethical Complications of Lynching: Ida B. Wells's Interrogation of American Terror* (New York: Palgrave Macmillan, 2010), 129.

58   Stewart E. Tolnay and E. M. Beck, *A Festival of Violence: An Analysis of Southern Lynchings, 1882–1930* (Urbana: University of Illinois Press, 1995), ix.

59   Hartsfield, interview by Sims, July 31, 2009.

60   Tolnay and Beck, *Festival of Violence*, 259–62.

61   W. Fitzhugh Brundage, *Lynching in the New South: Georgia and Virginia, 1880–1930* (Urbana: University of Illinois Press, 1993); Philip Dray, *At the Hands of Persons Unknown: The Lynching of Black America* (New York: Modern Library, 2003).

62   See selected works by Ralph Ginzburg, *100 Years of Lynchings* (Baltimore, Md.: Black Classic, 1962); Jonathan Markovitz, *Legacies of Lynching: Racial Violence and Memory* (Minneapolis: University of Minnesota Press, 2004); Arthur F. Raper, *The Tragedy of Lynching* (Mineola, N.Y.: Dover, 2003 [an unabridged republication of the work originally published in 1933 by the University of North Carolina Press, Chapel Hill]); and Christopher Waldrep, ed., *Lynching in America: A History in Documents* (New York: New York University Press, 2006).

63   Note Isabel Wilkerson's 2010 publication *The Warmth of Other Suns: The Epic Story of American's Great Migration* (New York: Random House, 2010).

64   Stellar examples are Ida B. Wells and Walter White.

65 Abel Meeropol, writing under the pseudonym Allan Lewis, captured the essence of what several historians term, and correctly so, the United States' national crime. Written during a period marked by southern flight, and memorialized by Billie Holliday's "haunting 1939 rendition," lynching (bullet-pierced, charred, decapitated bodies of black people) is still a moral problem in the United States. See "Strange Fruit," PBS, http://www.pbs.org/independentlens/strangefruit/film.html (accessed December 22, 2015).

66 See Michelle Alexander, *The New Jim Crow: Mass Incarceration in the Age of Colorblindness* (New York: New Press, 2010).

67 Hartsfield, interview by Sims, July 31, 2009.

3: Faithful Witness

1 Black prophetic practices, according to Cornel West, "best exemplify the truncated content and character of American prophetic practices; they reveal the strengths and shortcomings, the importance and impotence, of prophetic activities in recalcitrant America. Black prophetic practices assume that—after the most intense scrutiny—some ultimate sense of a morally grounded sense of justice ought to prevail in personal and societal affairs." West, "The Prophetic Tradition in Afro-America," in *African American Religious Thought*, ed. Cornel West and Eddie S. Glaude Jr. (Louisville, Ky.: Westminster John Knox, 2003), 1040.

2 For information on how particular experiential accounts are received, see Thomas Trezise, *Witnessing Witnessing: On the Reception of Holocaust Survivor Testimony* (New York: Fordham University Press, 2013).

3 See Rosetta E. Ross, *Witnessing & Testifying: Black Women, Religion and Civil Rights* (Minneapolis: Augsburg Fortress, 2003), chs. 1 and 6; Antipas Harris, "We Overcome by the Word of Our Testimony: 'Anybody Got a Testimony?'"

Renewal Dynamics (blog), February 25, 2014, http://renewal dynamics.com/2014/02/25/we-overcome-by-the-word-of -our-testimony/; Daphne C. Wiggins, *Righteous Content: Black Women's Perspectives of Church and Faith* (New York: New York University Press, 2005), ch. 2.

4   Psalm 137:4.

5   The deaths of Tamir Rice and John Crawford draw attention to an aspect of neo-lynching culture whereby children and adults alike are presumed guilty of something and denied a right to speak on their own behalf as some on-duty police officers operate from a position of shoot first and inquire later. For responses to this disturbing trend, see Patricia Lefevere, "Theologians Speak Out on Racism," *National Catholic Reporter*, January 16, 2015, 17; Marc H. Morial, "From the President's Desk," *National Urban League: The State of Black America*, January 1, 2015; Ryan Herring, "Hands Up! Don't Shoot!" *Sojourners Magazine*, November 2014; "Ohio Deaths Renew Calls for Lookalike Guns Action," *St Louis Post-Dispatch (MO)*, December 8, 2014; Patrik Jonsson, "'Black Man with a Gun' Author Explains Why He Doesn't Carry One," *Christian Science Monitor*, December 13, 2014.

6   See Radley Balko, "Welcome to the Police Industrial Complex," *Huffington Post*, June 19, 2013, http://www.huffingtonpost .com/2013/06/19/welcome-to-the-police-ind_n_3415442 .html; idem., *Rise of the Warrior Cop: The Militarization of America's Police Forces* (New York: Public Affairs, 2013); Jim Fisher, *SWAT Madness and the Militarization of the American Police: A National Dilemma* (Santa Barbara, Calif.: Praeger, 2010); Abigail R. Hall and Christopher J. Coyne, "The Militarization of US Domestic Policing," *Independent Review* 17, no. 4 (2013): 485–504; and John W. Whitehead, *A Government of Wolves: The Emerging American Police State* (New York: SelectBooks, 2013).

7   "ACLU on 'The Militarization of American Policing,'" *Homeland Security Digital Library* (blog), August 14, 2014, https://www

.hsdl.org/blog/newpost/view/aclu-on-the-militarization-of
-american-policing; and Hank Johnson, "More Must Be Done
to De-militarize Our Police," *Huffington Post*, June 4, 2015,
http://www.huffingtonpost.com/rep-hank-johnson/-more
-must-be-done-to-de_b_7512526.html.

8   See "Geneva Conventions and Commentaries," International Committee of the Red Cross, https://www.icrc.org/
en/war-and-law/treaties-customary-law/geneva-conventions
(accessed December 23, 2015); Amitai Etzioni, "Rules of
Engagement and Abusive Citizens," *Prism: A Journal of the
Center for Complex Operations* 4, no. 4 (2013): 87–102;
Graham Day and Christopher Freeman, "Operationalizing
the Responsibility to Protect—the Policekeeping Approach,"
Global Governance 11, no. 2 (2005): 139–46; Stephen Hill
and Randall Beger, "A Paramilitary Policing Juggernaut,"
Social Justice 36, no. 1 (2009): 25–40.

9   For information on the creation of intentional all-white
communities, see James W. Loewen, *Sundown Towns: A
Hidden Dimension of American Racism* (New York: New
Press, 2005); "Sundown Towns: Aka Racial Cleansing,"
Encyclopedia of Arkansas History & Culture, http://www
.encyclopediaofarkansas.net/encyclopedia/entry-detail.aspx
?entryid=3658 (accessed December 23, 2005); and Ronda
Racha Penrice, "'Sundown Towns' under a Spotlight in New
Investigation Discovery Documentary," *theGrio*, February
25, 2014, http://thegrio.com/2014/02/25/sundown-towns
-under-a-spotlight-in-new-investigation-discovery-documen
tary/ (accessed December 23, 2015).

10 Lois-Louise Miller, interview by Angela D. Sims, February 23,
2011, in Dallas, Tex., transcript, Baylor University Institute
for Oral History, Waco, Tex., available online at http://digital
collections.baylor.edu/cdm/ref/collection/buioh/id/6641.

11 Nottingham, interview by Sims, August 26, 2009.

12 Fletcher, interview by Sims, August 31, 2009.

13 Hardimon, interview by Sims, March 4, 2010.

14   Ideally, any person suspected of a crime should be arrested without fatal results. Yet the treatment of white men who are arrested for murder raises serious concerns about what presents as preferential treatment for a select group of people. For example, see Jason Sickles, "Dylann Roof Arrest Video Reveals Officers' Emotions after Capturing Charleston Murder Suspect," Yahoo, June 23, 2015, http://news.yahoo .com/dylann-roof-arrest-video-reveals-officers-relished -capturing-charleston-murder-suspect-003707280.html; and Lindsey Bever and Abby Ohlheiser, "Captured: Eric Matthew Frein, Alleged Cop Killer and 'Most Wanted' Fugitive," *Washington Post*, October 31, 2014, https://www.washingtonpost .com/news/morning-mix/wp/2014/10/31/pennsylvania -police-have-suspected-cop-killer-eric-frein-in-custody/.

15   Although there are questions about the origin of "hands up, don't shoot," its implied meaning may not be as obvious as it is to persons who live in communities that are subjected to intense police scrutiny. For varied perspectives see Cheryl Corley, "Whether History or Hype, 'Hands Up, Don't Shoot' Endures," NPR, August 8, 2015, http://www .npr.org/2015/08/08/430411141/whether-history-or -hype-hands-up-dont-shoot-endures; "Considering Police Body Cameras," *Harvard Law Review* 128, no. 6 (2015): 1794–1817; William F. Jasper, "Are Local Police to Blame? With Riots and Killings Happening in Cities in the Wake of the Deaths of Young Black Men, Political Elites Are Calling for Nationalizing Local Police, but What Would That Actually Do?" *New American*, September 21, 2015.

16   Hannah White Allen, interview by Angela D. Sims, March 5, 2010, in Oklahoma City, Okla., transcript, Baylor University Institute for Oral History, Waco, Tex., available online at http://digitalcollections.baylor.edu/cdm/ref/collection/ buioh/id/6593; Albert David Anderson, interview by Angela D. Sims, October 28, 2009, in Sumter, S.C., transcript, Baylor University Institute for Oral History, Waco, Tex., available

online at http://digitalcollections.baylor.edu/cdm/ref/collection/buioh/id/6594; Parks, interview by Sims, August 18, 2009; Arthur Dunn, interview by Angela D. Sims, January 13, 2010, in Oakland, Calif., transcript, Baylor University Institute for Oral History, Waco, Tex., available online at http://digitalcollections.baylor.edu/cdm/ref/collection/buioh/id/6609; Fletcher, interview by Sims, August 31, 2009; Emma Atkins Kidd, interview by Angela D. Sims, August 18, 2009, in Benton, La., transcript, Baylor University Institute for Oral History, Waco, Tex., available online at http://digital collections.baylor.edu/cdm/ref/collection/buioh/id/6612; Clark, interview by Sims, November 24, 2009; Collins, interview by Sims, August 20, 2009; Franklin, interview by Sims, August 18, 2009; Gay, interview by Sims, September 4, 2009; Hardimon, interview by Sims, March 4, 2010; Hill, interview by Sims, January 13, 2010; Cudjoe, interview by Sims, March 4, 2010; Hunter, interview by Sims, March 4, 2010; Jones, interview by Sims, December 28, 2009.

17 Anderson, interview by Sims, October 28, 2009.

18 Parks, interview by Sims, August 18, 2009.

19 See "A Partial Listing of Approximately 5,000 Negroes Lynched in United States since 1859" in Ralph Ginzburg, *100 Years of Lynchings* (Baltimore, Md.: Black Classic, 1962, 1988), 262.

20 John Andrew Prime, "Lynchings' Bloody Terror Toll Studied," *Times* (Shreveport), February 16, 2015, http://www.shreveporttimes.com/story/news/local/2015/02/15/lynchings-bloody-terror-toll-studied/23458327/.

21 Parks, interview by Sims, August 18, 2009.

22 Solon Marshall, interview by Angela D. Sims, August 13, 2009, in Winnsboro, La., transcript, Baylor University Institute for Oral History, Waco, Tex., available online at http://digital collections.baylor.edu/cdm/ref/collection/buioh/id/6637.

23 Zan Wesley Holmes Jr., interview by Angela D. Sims, February 22, 2011, in Dallas, Tex., transcript, Baylor University Institute

for Oral History, Waco, Tex., available online at http://digital collections.baylor.edu/cdm/ref/collection/buioh/id/7017.

24   Holmes, interview by Sims, February 22, 2011.

25   Ola Mae Jackson Comins, interview by Angela D. Sims, February 24, 2011, in Dallas, Tex., transcript, Baylor University Institute for Oral History, Waco, Tex., available online at http://digitalcollections.baylor.edu/cdm/ref/collection/buioh/id/6604.

26   C. W. Kidd and Parks, interview by Angela D. Sims, August 18, 2009.

27   See "Oklahoma Land Run," Oklahoma Historical Society, http://www.okhistory.org/kids/lrexhibit (accessed December 23, 2015); "Land Run of 1889," Oklahoma Historical Society, http://www.okhistory.org/publications/enc/entry.php?entry=LA014 (accessed December 23, 2015).

28   "Lynching," Oklahoma Historical Society, http://www.okhistory.org/publications/enc/entry.php?entry=LY001 (accessed December 23, 2015).

29   Hardimon, interview by Sims, March 4, 2010. For information on black life in Tulsa, before and after the 1921 riot, see John Hope Franklin, *Mirror to America: The Autobiography of John Hope Franklin* (New York: Farrar, Straus & Giroux, 2005). For information on Tulsa's race riot, see Tim Madigan, *The Burning: Massacre, Destruction, and the Tulsa Race Riot of 1921* (New York: St. Martin's, 2001); Chris M. Messer, "The Tulsa Race Riot of 1921: Toward an Integrative Theory of Collective Violence," *Journal of Social History* 44, no. 4 (2011): 1217–32.

30   Hardimon, interview by Sims, March 4, 2010.

31   Brad A. Myrstol, "Public Perceptions of School Resource Officer (SRO) Programs," *Western Criminology Review* 12, no. 3 (2011): 20-40.

32   Hardimon, interview by Sims, March 4, 2010.

33   Jerome Karabel, "Police Killings Surpass the Worst Years of Lynching, Capital Punishment, and a Movement

Responds," *Huffington Post*, November 4, 2015, http://
www.huffingtonpost.com/jerome-karabel/police-killings
-lynchings-capital-punishment_b_8462778.html?utm_hp
_ref=black-voices&ir=Black%20Voices&utm_hp_ref
=black-voices.

34 E. A. Kidd and Parks, interview by Sims, August 18, 2009.

35 Hardimon, interview by Sims, March 4, 2010.

36 Clark, interview by Sims, November 24, 2009.

37 Collins, interview by Sims, August 20, 2009.

38 For information on Saint Joseph, Missouri, see Preston Fil-
bert, *The Half Not Told: The Civil War in a Frontier Town*
(Mechanicsburg, Pa.: Stackpole Books, 2001); Sheridan
A. Logan, *Old Saint Jo: Gateway to the West, 1799–1932*
(St. Joseph, Mo.: Platte Purchase Publishers, A Division of the
St. Joseph Museums, 2002); "History of St. Joseph," official
website of St. Joseph, http://www.stjoemo.info/index.aspx
?nid=151 (accessed December 23, 2015).

39 Fletcher would have been fifteen years old and more than
likely in tenth grade when nineteen-year-old Lloyd Warner
was lynched on November 28, 1933, which she remembered
taking place in 1931.

40 While Fletcher's recollection of actual dates differs from documented sources, this should in no way diminish her recounting
of lynching as an act of domestic terror. For information on a
1931 lynching in Maryville, Mo., see "1931 Maryville, Missouri
Lynching . . . ," Timothy Hughes Rare & Early Newspapers,
http://www.rarenewspapers.com/view/569801   (accessed
December 23, 2015); "Colter-Gunn Incident Bibliography,"
Northwest Missouri State University, http://www.nwmissouri
.edu/library/courses/history/COLTERGUNN.HTM (accessed
December 23, 2015); Amy Louise Wood, *Lynching and Spectacle: Witnessing Racial Violence in America, 1890–1940*
(Chapel Hill: University of North Carolina Press, 2009), 306.

41 Born in 1918, Fletcher was thirteen when Raymond Gunn was
lynched.

42 Fletcher, interview by Sims, August 31, 2009.

43 James W. Drakeford Sr., interview by Angela D. Sims, July 15, 2009, in Ashland, Va., transcript, Baylor University Institute for Oral History, Waco, Tex., available online at http://digital collections.baylor.edu/cdm/ref/collection/buioh/id/6608.

44 See Joan A. Inabinet and L. Glen Inabinet, *A History of Kershaw County, South Carolina* (Columbia: University of South Carolina Press, 2011).

45 Drakeford, interview by Sims, July 15, 2009. For a description of "Uncle Tom," see Riché Richardson, *Black Masculinity and the US South: From Uncle Tom to Gangsta* (Athens: University of Georgia Press, 2007).

46 Drakeford, interview by Sims, July 15, 2009.

47 Drakeford, interview by Sims, July 15, 2009.

48 See Gwendolyn Parris Swinton, Dedra S. Arthur, and Haroldine T. Parris, *The History of Central Colored High School* (Dallas: Memories Publishing, 1996).

49 Joseph, interview by Sims, January 16, 2010.

50 Joseph, interview by Sims, January 16, 2010.

51 C. W. Kidd, interview by Sims, August 18, 2009.

52 Margie Kidd Campbell, interview by Angela D. Sims, August 18, 2009, in Benton, La., transcript, Baylor University Institute for Oral History, Waco, Tex., available online at http://digitalcollections.baylor.edu/cdm/ref/collection/buioh/id/6612.

53 James Allen and John Lewis, *Without Sanctuary: Lynching Photography in America* (Santa Fe, N.Mex.: Twin Palms, 2000).

54 E. A. Kidd, interview by Sims, August 18, 2009.

55 C. W. Kidd, interview by Sims, August 18, 2009.

56 Odell Carr, interview by Angela D. Sims, July 14, 2009, in Woodbridge, Va., transcript, Baylor University Institute for Oral History, Waco, Tex., available online at http://digital collections.baylor.edu/cdm/ref/collection/buioh/id/6600.

57 Drakeford, interview by Sims, July 15, 2009.

58 Earl Williams Sr., interview by Angela D. Sims, November 24, 2009, in Linden, N.J., transcript, Baylor University Institute for Oral History, Waco, Tex., available online at http://digital collections.baylor.edu/cdm/ref/collection/buioh/id/6632.

4: Unrelenting Tenacity

1 This song captures the essence of Ella Baker's commitment to civil rights. See "Ella's Song: 'We Who Believe in Freedom Cannot Rest until It Comes,'" Ella Baker Center for Human Rights, http://ellabakercenter.org/blog/2013/12/ellas-song-we -who-believe-in-freedom-cannot-rest-until-it-comes (accessed December 24, 2015).

2 Scripture, tradition, reason, and experience are typically referred to as primary resources for Christian ethics. An unquestioned acceptance of European thinkers and philo- sophical worldviews as foundational sources often results in a further diminishment of counter or even complementary views.

3 For instance, Amy Kate Bailey and Stewart E. Tolnay, *Lynched: The Victims of Southern Mob Violence* (Chapel Hill: Univer- sity of North Carolina Press, 2015); Stewart E. Tolnay and E. M. Beck, *A Festival of Violence: An Analysis of Southern Lynchings, 1882–1930* (Urbana: University of Illinois Press, 1995).

4 See Isabel Wilkerson, "Mike Brown's Shooting and Jim Crow Lynchings Have Too Much in Common: It's Time for America to Own Up," *Guardian*, August 25, 2014, http:// www.theguardian.com/commentisfree/2014/aug/25/mik -brown-shooting-jim-crow-lynchings-in-common; William C. Anderson, "From Lynching Photos to Michael Brown's Body: Commodifying Black Death," *Truthout*, January 16, 2015, http://www.truth-out.org/news/item/28580-from-lynching -photos-to-michael-brown-s-body-commodifying-black -death.

5   For information about this 2011 phenomenon that was her-
    alded by many journalists in the United States as a remarkable
    response to tyranny, see Mark L. Haas and David W. Lesch,
    eds., *The Arab Spring: Change and Resistance in the Middle
    East* (Boulder, Colo.: Westview, 2012); Dafna Hochman Rand,
    *Roots of the Arab Spring: Contested Authority and Political
    Change in the Middle East* (Philadelphia: University of Penn-
    sylvania Press, 2013); Gamal M. Selim, "The United States
    and the Arab Spring: The Dynamics of Political Engineering,"
    Arab Studies Quarterly 35, no. 3 (2013): 255–72; Paul R. Wil-
    liams and Colleen Popken, "US Foreign Policy and the Arab
    Spring: Ten Short-Term Lessons Learned," *Denver Journal of
    International Law and Policy* 41, no. 1 (2012): 47–61.

6   For advice Palestinians offered to Ferguson protesters, see
    Robert Mackey, "Advice for Ferguson's Protesters from the
    Middle East," *New York Times*, August 14, 2014, http://www
    .nytimes.com/2014/08/15/world/middleeast/advice-for
    -fergusons-protesters-from-the-middle-east.html?_r=0;
    Bassem Masri, "The Fascinating Story of How the Ferguson-
    Palestine Solidarity Movement Came Together," AlterNet, Feb-
    ruary 18, 2015, http://www.alternet.org/activism/frontline
    -ferguson-protester-and-palestinian-american-bassem-masri
    -how-ferguson2palestine.

7   Habakkuk 1:2 NRSV.

8   "Crime in Philadelphia," *Philadelphia Inquirer*, http://data
    .inquirer.com/crime/neighborhood/southwest-philadelphia/
    (accessed December 24, 2015); for additional information on
    this section of Philadelphia, see Anne E. Krulikowski, "South-
    west Philadelphia," *Encyclopedia of Greater Philadelphia*,
    http://philadelphiaencyclopedia.org/archive/southwest
    -philadelphia-essay/ (accessed December 24, 2015).

9   Nottingham, interview by Sims, August 26, 2009.

10 See Albert J. Raboteau's seminal work, *Slave Religion: The
    "Invisible Institution" in the Antebellum South*, 2nd ed. (New
    York: Oxford University Press, 2004).

11 Nottingham, interview by Sims, August 26, 2009.

12 Kidd Campbell, interview by Sims, August 18, 2009.

13 Kidd Campbell, interview by Sims, August 18, 2009.

14 Dean, interview by Sims, February 13, 2010.

15 Gay, interview by Sims, September 4, 2009.

16 Lewis, interview by Sims, January 13, 2010.

17 Marigny, interview by Sims, March 5, 2010.

18 Helen Swazer Pollard, interview by Angela D. Sims, January 11, 2010, in Hayward, Calif., transcript, Baylor University Institute for Oral History, Waco, Tex., available online at http://digitalcollections.baylor.edu/cdm/ref/collection/buioh/id/6621.

19 Nottingham, interview by Sims, August 26, 2009.

20 KJV.

21 Holmes, interview by Sims, February 22, 2011. Holmes ran for the unexpired term of Joseph E. Lockridge, who died in an airplane crash. See "Lockridge, Joseph Edwin," Texas State Historical Association, https://tshaonline.org/handbook/online/articles/flo53 (accessed December 24, 2015); "Joseph E. Lockridge," Legislative Reference Library of Texas, http://www.lrl.state.tx.us/mobile/memberdisplay.cfm?memberID=829 (accessed December 24, 2015); Alwyn Barr, *Black Texans: A History of African Americans in Texas, 1598–1925* (Norman: University of Oklahoma Press, 2002), 179–80.

22 Holmes, interview by Sims, February 22, 2011.

23 For information on this May 15, 1916, event, see Patricia Bernstein, *The First Waco Horror: The Lynching of Jesse Washington and the Rise of the NAACP* (College Station: Texas A&M University Press, 2005); "Jesse Washington Lynching," Texas State Historical Assocation, https://tshaonline.org/handbook/online/articles/jcj01 (accessed December 24, 2015); Wade Goodwyn, "Waco Recalls a 90-Year-Old 'Horror,'" NPR, May 13, 2006, http://www.npr.org/templates/story/story.php?storyId=5401868; Kurt Terry, "Jesse

Washington Lynching," Waco History, http://wacohistory. org/items/show/55 (accessed December 24, 2015).

24 Holmes, interview by Sims, February 22, 2011.

25 Holmes, interview by Sims, February 22, 2011.

26 For information on St. Luke "Community" United Methodist Church, see http://slcumc.org/about-us/church-history (accessed May 2, 2016).

27 Holmes, interview by Sims, February 22, 2011.

28 Walker, interview by Sims, March 5, 2010.

29 Thomas Arthur Ballard, interview by Angela D. Sims, January 12, 2010, in Hayward, Calif., transcript, Baylor University Institute for Oral History, Waco, Tex., available online at http://digitalcollections.baylor.edu/cdm/ref/collection/buioh/id/6596.

30 Purvis, interview by Sims, February 13, 2010.

31 Johnson, interview by Sims, February 23, 2011.

32 Clark, interview by Sims, November 24, 2009.

33 Williams, interview by Sims, November 24, 2009.

34 Lewis, interview by Sims, January 13, 2010; Lewis was almost three years old when Bonnie and Clyde were killed by Bienville Parish sheriffs. See "History," Town of Arcadia, Louisiana, http://www.arcadialouisiana.org/arcadialouisiana/History .html (accessed December 1, 2015). Of particular concern is the manner in which Arcadia has commercialized and glamorized criminal behavior. See "Bonnie & Clyde," Town of Arcadia, Louisiana, http://www.arcadialouisiana.org/arcadialouisiana/Bonnie%26Clyde.html (accessed December 1, 2015).

35 It is quite possible that Dr. Lewis is referring to the October 13, 1938, lynching of W. C. Williams in Lincoln Parish. See the June 13, 2005, Congressional Record, vol. 151, no. 77, at http://www.gpo.gov/fdsys/pkg/CREC-2005-06-13/html/CREC-2005-06-13-pt1-PgS6364-3.htm (accessed December 24, 2015); see also "Ruston, Louisiana Lynching . . . ," Timothy Hughes Rare & Early Newspapers, http://www.rarenewspapers.com/view/573065 (accessed December 24, 2015);

"The Lynching of W. C. or R. C. Williams," Without Sanctuary, http://withoutsanctuary.org/pics_73.html (accessed December 24, 2015).

36 Lewis, interview by Sims, January 13, 2010.

37 Lewis, interview by Sims, January 13, 2010.

38 Clark, interview by Sims, November 24, 2009.

39 Purvis, interview by Sims, February 13, 2010.

40 Hardimon, interview by Sims, March 4, 2010.

41 Of particular concern are views espoused by Senator Ted Cruz and Mr. Donald Trump, whose rhetoric advances hatred and fear as a mechanism to incite hysteria. For examples, see David Sherfinski, "Ted Cruz: 'You Don't Stop Bad Guys by Taking Away Our Guns,'" *Washington Times*, December 7, 2015, http://www.washingtontimes.com/news/2015/dec/7/ ted-cruz-you-dont-stop-bad-guys-taking-away-our-gu/; Ed Pilkington, "Donald Trump: Ban All Muslims Entering US," *Guardian*, December 7, 2015, http://www.theguardian .com/us-news/2015/dec/07/donald-trump-ban-all-muslims -entering-us-san-bernardino-shooting.

42 Marshall, interview by Sims, August 13, 2009.

43 Pollard, interview by Sims, January 11, 2010.

44 Dorothy Thomas, interview by Angela D. Sims, March 4, 2010, in Oklahoma City, Okla., transcript, Baylor University Institute for Oral History, Waco, Tex., available online at http:// digitalcollections.baylor.edu/cdm/ref/collection/buioh/ id/6628.

45 Myrtle Ethel Ballard, interview by Angela D. Sims, January 12, 2010, in Hayward, Calif., transcript, Baylor University Institute for Oral History, Waco, Tex., available online at http:// digitalcollections.baylor.edu/cdm/ref/collection/buioh/ id/6596.

46 Alex Mikulich, "The Death Penalty in Dixie: The Enduring Legacy of the Confederate Flag and Racism," Loyola University New Orleans, http://www.loyno.edu/jsri/death-penalty -dixie (accessed December 9, 2015).

47   Ballard, interview by Sims, January 12, 2010. While a record of this event is not included in the Congressional Record (http://www.gpo.gov/fdsys/pkg/CREC-2005-06-13/html/CREC-2005-06-13-pt1-PgS6364-3.htm [accessed December 24, 2015]) and while I was unable to obtain a copy of the *Shreveport Sun*, the oldest weekly newspaper for African Americans in Louisiana, there are documented accounts of black veterans who were lynched while in their uniform. See, e.g., Dora Apel, *Imagery of Lynching: Black Men, White Women, and the Mob* (New Brunswick, N.J.: Rutgers University Press, 2004), 174; William G. Jordan, *Black Newspapers and America's War for Democracy, 1914–1920* (Chapel Hill: University of North Carolina Press, 2001).

48   Ballard, interview by Sims, January 12, 2010.

49   Carr, interview by Sims, July 14, 2009.

50   Simon Morgan, interview by Angela D. Sims, July 14, 2009, in Woodbridge, Va., transcript, Baylor University Institute for Oral History, Waco, Tex., available online at http://digitalcollections.baylor.edu/cdm/ref/collection/buioh/id/6642.

51   Ephesians 6:12b.

5: Lessons, Concerns, Hopes

1   Collins, interview by Sims, August 20, 2009.

2   Collins, interview by Sims, August 20, 2009.

3   Collins, interview by Sims, August 20, 2009.

4   I shared this observation with Dr. Freddie Cudjoe. See Cudjoe, interview by Sims, March 4, 2010.

5   Davis, interview by Sims, March 4, 2010.

6   Paraphrase of Theresa Gilliam's comment "What you are to be you are now becoming." Theresa Jackson Gilliam, interview by Angela D. Sims, December 28, 2009, in Lake Charles, La., transcript, Baylor University Institute for Oral History, Waco, Tex., available online at http://digitalcollections.baylor.edu/cdm/ref/collection/buioh/id/7014.

7   Carr, interview by Sims, July 14, 2009.

8   Lewis, interview by Sims, January 13, 2010.

9   Allen, interview by Sims, March 5, 2010.

10 Marguerite Harris, interview by Angela D. Sims, July 10, 2009, in Woodbridge, Va., transcript, Baylor University Institute for Oral History, Waco, Tex., available online at http://digital collections.baylor.edu/cdm/ref/collection/buioh/id/6597.

11 Clark, interview by Sims, November 24, 2009.

12 George Hampton, interview by Angela D. Sims, July 10, 2009, in Woodbridge, Va., transcript, Baylor University Institute for Oral History, Waco, Tex., available online at http://digital collections.baylor.edu/cdm/ref/collection/buioh/id/6597.

13 Born in 1928, Hampton would have been sixteen or seventeen when he left Englewood, New Jersey. If his mother died when he was fifteen, Hampton moved to Greensboro, North Carolina, in 1943 or 1944, not 1945.

14 Hampton, interview by Sims, July 10, 2009.

15 I asked this follow-up question in response to George Hampton's comment about dual standards applicable to black people. See Hampton, interview by Sims, July 10, 2009.

16 Hampton, interview by Sims, July 10, 2009.

17 Pollard, interview by Sims, January 11, 2010.

18 John Jones, interview by Angela D. Sims, July 10, 2009, in Woodbridge, Va., transcript, Baylor University Institute for Oral History, Waco, Tex., available online at http://digital collections.baylor.edu/cdm/ref/collection/buioh/id/6597.

19 Clark, interview by Sims, November 24, 2009.

20 Clark, interview by Sims, November 24, 2009.

21 Marshall, interview by Sims, August 13, 2009.

22 Harris, interview by Sims, July 10, 2009.

23 Here I refer to Justice Antonin Scalia's comments regarding admissions policies at the University of Texas in Austin. For responses to his remarks about black intellectual inferiority see Afi-Odelia Scruggs, "Dear Justice Scalia: Here's What I LearnedasaBlackStudentStrugglingatanEliteCollege," *Wash-*

ington Post, December 11, 2015, https://www.washington
post.com/news/grade-point/wp/2015/12/11/dear-justice
-scalia-heres-what-i-learned-as-a-black-student-struggling
-at-an-elite-college/; Ariane De Vogue, "Supreme Court
Releases Audio of Justice Antonin Scalia Saying Maybe Black
Students Don't Belong at Elite Universities," CNN, December 11, 2015, http://www.cnn.com/2015/12/11/politics/
supreme-court-antonin-scalia-african-americans-audio/.

24 Clark, interview by Sims, November 24, 2009.

25 Pollard, interview by Sims, January 11, 2010.

26 Pollard, interview by Sims, January 11, 2010.

27 Allen, interview by Sims, March 5, 2010.

28 Harris, interview by Sims, July 16, 2009.

29 Morgan, interview by Sims, July 14, 2009.

30 This quote, attributed to J. Edgar Hoover, former director of
the Federal Bureau of Investigations, raised significant concerns during the 1970s when the Black Panthers were subjected to increased scrutiny by law enforcement agencies. See
the J. Edgar Hoover Foundation website, http://www.jedgar
hooverfoundation.org (accessed December 24, 2015). For an
examination of this rhetoric as a designator for racism, see
John Hagan, "Law, Order and Sentencing: A Study of Attitude
in Action," *Sociometry* 38, no. 3 (1975): 374–84.

31 Anderson, interview by Sims, October 28, 2009.

32 Allen, interview by Sims, March 5, 2010.

33 Corbin, interview by Sims, August 13, 2009.

34 Blunt, interview by Sims, August 13, 2009.

35 C. W. Kidd, interview by Sims, August 18, 2009.

36 Parks, interview by Sims, August 18, 2009.

37 C. W. Kidd, interview by Sims, August 18, 2009.

38 Dean, interview by Sims, February 13, 2010; Fletcher, interview by Sims, August 31, 2009; Anderson, interview by Sims,
October 28, 2009; Miller, interview by Sims, February 23,
2011.

39 Ephesians 6:10.

40 Carr, interview by Sims, July 14, 2009.

41 Richard Kluger, *Simple Justice: The History of Brown v. Board of Education and America's Struggle for Equality* (New York: Vintage, 2004); James T. Patterson, *Brown v. Board of Education: A Civil Rights Milestone and Its Troubled Legacy* (New York: Oxford University Press, 2001); Ivory A. Toldson, "60 Years after *Brown v. Board of Education*: The Impact of the Congressional Black Caucus on the Education of Black People in the United States of America (Editor's Commentary)," *Journal of Negro Education* 83, no. 3 (2014): 194–98; James L. Moore and Chance W. Lewis, "Guest Editorial: 60 Years after *Brown v. Board of Education*: Educational Advancement or Decline?" *Journal of Negro Education* 83, no. 3 (2014): 191–93.

42 Elwood Ball, interview by Angela D. Sims, July 10, 2009, in Woodbridge, Va., transcript, Baylor University Institute for Oral History, Waco, Tex., available online at http://digital collections.baylor.edu/cdm/ref/collection/buioh/id/6597.

43 Hampton, interview by Sims, July 10, 2009.

44 Campbell, interview by Sims, August 18, 2009.

45 Hampton, interview by Sims, July 10, 2009.

46 Carr, interview by Sims, July 14, 2009.

47 Olive Lee Franklin, interview by Angela D. Sims, November 24, 2009, in Roselle, N.J., transcript, Baylor University Institute for Oral History, Waco, Tex., available online at http://digitalcollections.baylor.edu/cdm/ref/collection/buioh/id/6617.

48 Franklin, interview by Sims, November 24, 2009.

49 Hill, interview by Sims, September 17, 2009.

50 Randolph, interview by Sims, October 29, 2009.

51 Randolph, interview by Sims, October 29, 2009.

52 Holmes, interview by Sims, February 22, 2011.

53 Pollard, interview by Sims, January 11, 2010.

54 Fletcher, interview by Sims, August 31, 2009.

55 Fletcher, interview by Sims, August 31, 2009.

56 Hardimon, interview by Sims, March 4, 2010.

57 Parks, interview by Sims, August 18, 2009.

58 Morgan, interview by Sims, July 14, 2009.

59 Catherine T. Sidney, interview by Angela D. Sims, February 12, 2010, in Newport News, Va., transcript, Baylor University Institute for Oral History, Waco, Tex., available online at   http://digitalcollections.baylor.edu/cdm/ref/collection/buioh/id/6626.

60 Hardimon, interview by Sims, March 4, 2010.

61 Miller, interview by Sims, February 23, 2011; Pollard, interview by Sims, January 11, 2010; Sidney, interview by Sims, February 12, 2010.

Index